A PLUME BOOK

WOMEN'S LIBATION!

© Amy Buckley

Merrily Grashin is an illustrator and bartender living in Brooklyn. She runs a small business, Greet 'N' Potatoes, which produces cards and prints featuring food and beverage–themed illustrations and groanworthy jokes. She received her BA from NYU's Gallatin School with a concentration in community activism and political art theory. Merrily got her first job bussing tables at fifteen and has since worked in restaurants and bars across New York, from Bar Boulud on the Upper West Side to the Breslin in NoMad to Roberta's in Bushwick.

Women's Libation!

Cocktails to Celebrate a Woman's Right to Booze

Merrily Grashin

PLUME

PLUME
An imprint of Penguin Random House LLC
375 Hudson Street
New York, New York 10014

LIBRARY OF CONGRESS CATALOGING-IN-PUBLICATION DATA
Names: Grashin, Merrily, author.
Title: Women's libation! : cocktails to celebrate a woman's right to booze / Merrily Grashin.
Description: New York, New York : Plume, an imprint of Penguin Random House, LLC, [2017] | "A Plume Book." | Includes bibliographical references.
Identifiers: LCCN 2017025607 (print) | LCCN 2017036410 (ebook) | ISBN 9780735216938 (ebook) | ISBN 9780735216921 (tr)
Subjects: LCSH: Cocktails. | Alcoholic beverages. | LCGFT: Cookbooks.
Classification: LCC TX951 (ebook) | LCC TX951 .G694 2017 (print) | DDC 641.87/4—dc23
LC record available at https://lccn.loc.gov/2017025607

Printed in the United States of America
1   3   5   7   9   10   8   6   4   2

For Ellen Esposito and Mitch Grashin, best parents in the world.
(In my o-pun-ion.)

CONTENTS

GIN

VODKA

TEQUILA & MEZCAL

RUM

BRANDY & COGNAC

WINE, BEER & CIDER

OTHER SPIRITS

INTRODUCTION

This is precisely *the time when artists go to work. There is no time for despair, no place for self-pity, no need for silence, no room for fear. We speak, we write, we do language. That is how civilizations heal.*

—Toni Morrison

If you believe all sexes are equal, you're a feminist. It's as simple as that. My understanding of feminism is born out of the radical notion that women and men are entitled to equal rights—that regardless of our gender, we are all inherently limitless in our intellectual and physical agency. I'm a feminist because feminism is inviting. It's inclusive. It's intuitive. Feminism just makes sense.

Every time I read the news, with its increasingly misogynistic rhetoric, it feels more relevant and necessary than ever before to remember and honor the stories of the trailblazers: the brave women who have dedicated their lives to fighting for a voice and the movements that have laid a foundation for obtaining equal rights. They didn't ask for equal rights—asking would imply the rights were someone else's to give. They used their platforms, their skills, their positions, their adversities, and even their privileges to demand the rights that all people deserve.

This book is meant to celebrate those triumphs and honor those struggles by raising a glass. Or a few. Gathered here are a collection of some of the most beloved classic cocktails of all time, each one dedicated to one of these badass women or moments in the history of women's liberation—and most with a slight variation on the well-known classic recipe, giving small nods to each distinct story. I can't think of a better way to pay homage to your heroes than by getting totally drunk in their honor!

If you're not ovary-reacting (or, I should say, reacting with rational, moral sensibility), you're not paying attention!

For me, highlighting the singular and distinct struggles that make up our history has reinforced the importance of intersectionality in the fight for equal rights. Fighting for the rights of women means nothing if you're not fighting for the rights of people of all gender expressions, races, religions, sexualities, ethnicities, socioeconomic statuses, and abilities. If you share the goal of total equality, then examining the ways in which women are differently positioned or privileged can help to understand these divisions. We need to have one another's backs by giving credence to everyone's struggles, no matter how closely they mirror our own. And if we all get on the same page, we can come together and drink about it until we're so drunk and inspired that not only will we want to dismantle oppressive systems but there's also a good chance we'll want to sing karaoke.

Being a woman is a huge part of my identity and something I wanted to celebrate by creating this book that celebrates women. I wouldn't be standing here (or, more accurately, *sitting* here, drink in hand) with the opportunity to write this book without these fierce ladies before me. Their stories have helped me understand my own place in the shared and collective narrative . . . and given me a whole lot of good material for the next time I pull up a barstool or throw a cocktail party. More than anything, they make me want to raise a glass!

———

I've worked in bars and restaurants since my first job bussing tables at fifteen. For more than a decade in New York City, I've held almost every position within almost every type of establishment, from a fine-dining restaurant where I poured thirty-dollar glasses of Chardonnay from Bâtard-Montrachet; to a Brooklyn pizza joint operating out of a converted warehouse where I tested which cocktails, beer, and wine paired well with pizza (spoiler alert: they all do); to an English gastropub where I learned how to carve a suckling pig tableside and make a perfect Gin Martini; to your favorite dark bars where I poured whiskey shots and cracked cheap beers (and where you can find me when I'm off the clock).

Before the rush or on a slow night, I would scribble bad jokes and doodles, then pass them around for my coworkers to endure. I'd sketch the bottle of Aperol on the shelf and write underneath, "Aperol we've been through?!" handing it over as I implored them to take a shot with me. If halibut was on special, I would stand, arms held open with a drawing of a fish saying "Let's hug it out—just for the halibut." Food and, later, wine and spirits became my obsession; and so the collection grew. With the encouragement of my most inspiring and dysfunctional bar family, I started my greeting card line of food and beverage–themed puns called Greet 'N' Potatoes.

Flash forward two years and about two million bad pun ideas later, and I found myself sipping rosé-Aperol spritzers—what would become the "Rosé the Riveter" cocktail—and coming up with lists of punny cocktail names with a good friend, fellow pun-thusiast, and considerably mightier wordsmith than myself, Jane-Claire Quigley. Somewhere between rosé number two and, let's say . . . eight, there was a lightbulb moment: "What if all the cocktail names played off of badass women?!" "Ha-ha, like, feminist cocktails?" Yes. Exactly. Activism, social movements, art, influential women: this is what we had studied, read, cared about. Throw booze and bad jokes into the equation, and this book was for us and, the more I thought about it, a book for everyone.

And so, about five hundred scribbled puns and four hundred drinks later, this book was born.

I'm not sure that I would be able to write a cocktail book and feel comfortable exploring the craft if I hadn't spent years working in hospitality. I envisioned the book as an easy guide to making classic cocktails, with no bells and whistles and no need for prior craft-cocktail knowledge. This book is about passing on these recipes, but it's also about paying homage to my bar family: the seasoned bartenders who threw me to the lions on a busy Friday night while they took a smoke break, because they knew I could handle it; the managers who wrote me up for marking the wrong straws on certain cocktails but giggled about it over a post-work dice game and extra shift drink; the regulars who would bus glasses for me when I was too busy to do it myself but never ask for a free drink in return (obviously, I'd still comp them one).

———

I've had a lifelong enchantment with people who demand a space for themselves by forcing recognition—of their minds, bodies, stories—but not at the expense of others' comfort. What a cool way to walk through the world, knowing it's yours but, at the same time, that it doesn't belong to you, that it's meant to be shared. And this is how I think about my life in bars as well—both the ones I've stood behind and the ones I've built my nest in front of. It's the idea of having your "local." Your seat at the end of the bar that always seems to be warmed up for you. The bartenders who know your drink order before you sit down. The other regulars who have seen you in every state of happy or sad, and all the emotions (at all the intoxication levels) in between. You may not know their last name or what they do for work, but you know the way their head perks up when someone brings up the New York Mets or how their voice trembles when they talk about their childhood. You know their ex's biggest neuroses and turn-ons, though you've never met them in person or even caught their name. This is how we coexist, communicate, care for one another. How we evolve. We demand our space, but we share it with others.

I love the bar world that has helped raise me into a freethinking, strong woman (even if it's easy to sometimes forget how strong I really am). Writing this book has helped remind me of that, and the women we're raising a glass to have inspired me to keep creating. Even when it's easy to feel defeated (file under: current political climate), it's a way to facilitate an ongoing dialogue. In the tradition of radical pamphleteering (like the history—or many histories—within women's liberation movements), I wanted to make something to be shared, passed around, enjoyed, repeated. This is why I needed to make this book. To dedicate some of the greatest drinks of all time to some of the raddest ladies in history.

But I also just needed a place to put all those puns.

Cheers,
Merrily

THE ESSENTIALS

TOOLS OF THE TRADE

We'll get to the booze soon enough, but before anything else, a bartender needs to be outfitted with the right tools. Though we've all needed to get creative from time to time and been forced to mix up tipples with a butter knife in a pinch, being equipped with the right barware can go a long way toward creating consistent cocktails and improving the quality of your game. Here's an introductory set of suggestions to get you started.

Jigger (measuring cup for drinks): Most jiggers have two sides to measure different increments. While they come in many sizes, a good place to start is with one jigger that has a 1-ounce small cup and a 2-ounce large cup, and another that has a ¾-ounce small cup and a 1½-ounce large cup.

Mixing glass: A classic pint glass usually works just fine, but you can also find a hardy mixing glass designed for this sole purpose.

Shaker: A Boston shaker is best—the important part is the metal tin. These can have two metal parts, or the large half can be paired with a mixing glass, which is easily replaceable.

Strainers: A Hawthorne strainer is preferred—it has a flat top affixed to a coiled spring. These are commonly used for straining shaken drinks. Julep strainers are round, spoon-shaped strainers with no coil and are generally used for stirred drinks. If you're only going to opt for one for your home bar, however, go with the Hawthorne.

Bar spoon: These are long, slender spoons that help stir drinks without aerating the liquids too much.

Muddler: A dense wooden or metal tool used to crush or mix solid ingredients.

Peeler: A good peeler is a bartender's best friend when crafting the right garnish. A small, sharp knife works, but a Y-shaped peeler with the blade perpendicular to the handle is preferable. Make sure the blade is fresh!

Fresh ice: Make sure it tastes and smells, well, like nothing. This is *super* important. You wouldn't believe how much an ice tray that has been sitting next to your frozen chili for two weeks tastes like two-week-old frozen chili and how much it affects the taste of your drink. (It's definitely a bonus to have ice on the bigger side in most cases, since it melts less quickly and won't water down your drink, but size is nowhere near as important as freshness and purity.)

BREAKING THE GLASS CEILING ON GLASSWARE

No need to abide by conformist glassware suggestions! But, hey, just in case, here's a list for reference.

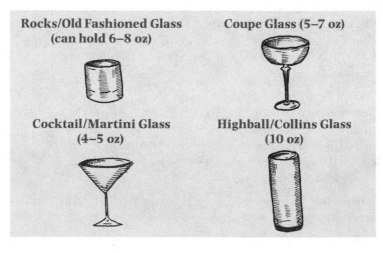

Rocks/Old Fashioned Glass (can hold 6–8 oz)

Coupe Glass (5–7 oz)

Cocktail/Martini Glass (4–5 oz)

Highball/Collins Glass (10 oz)

Flute (6 oz)

Wineglass (Bordeaux or Burgundy/White or Red) (varies)

Pint Glass (16 oz)

Hurricane Glass (20 oz)

Mug (Irish Coffee) (10 oz)

Cordial or Sherry Glass (4 oz)

(Brandy) Snifter (12 oz)

Shot Glass (2 oz)

CREATING YOUR PERFECT DRINK

Most cocktails, as with most everything in life, rely on a certain principle of balance. Begin with the understanding that your alcohol (spirit) is the star of the show. You want to both complement and emphasize its taste with a balance of the sweet (think sweet liqueurs, sugar, vermouth) and the more bold or even harsh flavors (think acidic citrus, bitters, herbal liqueurs). Of course, there are exceptions, but if you stick to this basic framework, it'll be easier not only to remember recipes but to experiment with making your own drinks. A good rule of thumb is that most classic cocktails have between 1½ and 3 ounces of total alcohol, in addition to a wide range of other components, mixers, and water.

BAR TIPS

Learning these simple terms will allow you to understand most basic drinks, streamline your techniques, and sound like a pro when whipping up your favorite cocktails at home.

"Build": If the cocktail calls for a "shake" or a "stir," you're generally meant to create, or "build," the drink in a separate mixing glass, which is then strained into its preferred glassware. This process helps evenly distribute the ingredients. It's good to get in the habit of building your cocktail using the same order of ingredients each time. I build mine from the bitters on up, which means I start with a dash of bitters (if the recipe calls for it), then the juices or syrups (the less vitally important, or cheaper, ingredients—this is in case you've made a mistake and need to start over; you can't be wasting that precious booze!). And, finally, I finish with the spirit or spirits. Some drinks are simple enough to be built directly in the glass (usually if there are only two parts or it's topped with a fizzy soda that can't be shaken), but others are more complex.

"Layer": Layered cocktails create a visible layering of ingredients and are often just for appearances. Sometimes the layering or separating of ingredients adds a complexity to the drink, allowing the tastes to evolve and change with each sip. Other times the layered drinks can be stirred after they've made their grand debut.

"Shake": Any drink that contains fruit juice, dairy, or eggs is generally meant to be shaken. To do this, fill your mixing glass with all ingredients, top with ice, and cover it with the shaker at a slight angle. Then tap the metal shaker with the heel of your hand until the two are sealed. Use both hands (especially if you're a beginner!) to shake it like hell.

"Stir": All drinks made solely from liquors and syrups should generally be stirred. In a mixing glass, build your cocktail (in the order you're in the habit of—bitters on up for me), fill the glass with ice, and stir gently with a bar spoon for about 15 seconds, until the drink is chilled and the ingredients are dispersed.

"Strain": Whether you're trying to separate your cocktail from the ice that chilled it, or you're trying to strain out ingredients you may have used while mixing (mint or muddled cherries, for example), using your strainer is key. It also minimizes mess by keeping the contents safe inside your mixing glass. To use a Hawthorne strainer (the one with the coil, which can be found at most kitchen or home-ware stores), place the flexible coils on the inside of the glass until the inner plate is flat on top, hold in place, and pour.

"Garnish": Often an oversight with home barkeeps, these finishing touches are integral to many drinks. Common garnishes such as lemon, orange, or lime wedges can allow the imbiber to adjust the flavors to their liking. Other garnishes like citrus twists and mint sprigs add a final touch of soft oils and aromas to a drink. Cherries and olives? Eating these is often one of the best parts of Martinis, Manhattans, and the like. Whatever the garnish, don't overlook it!

BAR TERMINOLOGY

Don't be intimidated by all the cocktail jargon spouted out at your local haunt! Here are some of the most useful ways to describe and modify your classic cocktails.

"Perfect": Believe it or not, there's not just one type of perfect in this world. Different standards of beauty, you say? Yes indeed! You can have a Perfect Martini or Perfect Manhattan. It just means instead of sticking to one type of vermouth (whichever the standard recipe calls for), you use equal parts sweet and dry. Yes, we can have it all!

"Dry": Less vermouth than the standard recipe calls for. So the less vermouth you use, the drier the Martini is considered to be. This has nothing to do with the type of vermouth being used (dry or sweet), just the amount.

"Very Dry"/"Extra Dry"/"Bone Dry": Just a whisper of vermouth, if any—a rinse of the glass works just fine. To most, an extra-dry Martini means you can probably just omit the vermouth altogether (when in doubt, just ask your Martini-loving pal to clarify their exact preference).

"Wet": Refers to the amount, or ratio, of vermouth to spirit. A wet Martini, for example, just refers to more vermouth than the recipe's standard.

"Dirty": The addition of a splash of olive juice (equal parts with your dry vermouth) to a Martini before mixing.

"Extra Dirty": The addition of a bigger splash of olive juice to a Martini.

"Up": In a chilled coupe or Martini glass. (Best if you get all riled "up" and demand your cocktail to be served cold and without ice!)

"On the Rocks": Served over ice.

"Neat": Served in a rocks glass with no ice.

ALCHEMY: Role of bitters, sugar, mixers, syrups, herbs & elixirs. (A nod to the history of alchemy and "stirring things up.")

Alchemy, essentially, is the process of mixing certain solutions or ingredients together to create or convert matter. Translation? Chemistry . . . or, ahem, cocktail-crafting (some even call it "mixology"), depending on how you look at it. The earliest records of Western female alchemists date back to the third century AD. Mary the Jewess and Cleopatra the Alchemist allegedly knew the formula to create the Philosopher's Stone, an elixir that could transform mercury into gold and provide longer, healthier lives—even immortality.

Now, I'm not saying the perfect Rye Manhattan has been known to produce similar results, but I'm also not *not* saying that. Alchemy is universal and noted in all recorded history, very often associated with the occult and magic. In essence, it's an evolving science of cause and effect, precision as well as improvisation, and sensitivity to the senses.

Mixing drinks is the same. It's art and science: when you measure correctly and with all variables in place, supposedly you can reproduce a consistent, perfect result. But so much is about experimentation, making mistakes, finding improvements, and personal preference. A Boulevardier probably wouldn't have come about if someone hadn't tried replacing gin with whiskey from one of the most iconic cocktails, the Negroni. Women wouldn't have earned their right to vote if courageous women like Susan B. Anthony hadn't tested and challenged the old-fashioned, unfair, and uncontested laws. Sure, that's not a perfect analogy, but the point is, change comes from observing the status quo, identifying and studying what works and what can be transformed, and then trying like hell to make something different, and maybe even better.

BITTERS, SYRUPS, SUGARS & CONCOCTIONS

Beyond the booze, there exists a dizzying array of modifiers and mixers in the world of bartending. From tiny little dash bottles to sticky-sweet syrups and exotic liquors, we love exploring all means of sprucing up your concoctions. This is by no means a definitive primer but rather an idea of some of the adjuncts you can work with.

Cocktail Bitters: The most common bitters you'll find (and the staple bottle for your personal bar) are Angostura Aromatic Bitters, though there are countless other brands and flavors available for you to experiment with. Bitters are a super-potent, heavily concentrated, high-alcohol extract of bitter roots, spices, seeds, fruits, and botanicals that are intended to change the flavor of the drink with just a dash or two. But you'd bitter not overdo it, or you may overpower the drink completely!

Bitter Liqueurs: Similar to cocktail bitters, bitter liqueurs (such as Campari, Amaro, and many herbal liqueurs) come in a wide variety of flavors and colors and are used to round out and enhance many of your drinks.

Infusions: For the sake of simplicity, we mostly avoid infusions for the classic recipes in this book; however, infusing base spirits with herbs, fruit, or spices is another super-easy way to flaunt your creativity at home. Depending on the potency of your additive, these can take minutes or days to finish . . . another opportunity to taste as you go.

Syrups: Many drinks call for simple syrup, which is just a fancy way to say sugar water. To make simple syrup, combine boiling hot water with a bunch of sugar. No need to be precise here—around equal parts is fine. White granulated sugar is the most common type used for simple syrup, but using unrefined or raw brown sugars creates a more toffee-like and slightly less sweet syrup. Homemade syrups offer an easy way to try on your alchemy hat and add new and distinct layers to many of the classics.

WHISKEY
(Bourbon, Rye, Scotch, Moonshine)

FIGHTING THE GOOD FIGHT

SMASH THE GOOD OLD FASHIONED PATRIARCHY!
(OLD FASHIONED)

The Old Fashioned is one of the most iconic and elemental cocktails of all time. In a way, it's an unsophisticated drink by cocktail standards: a simple mix of liquor, sugar, and bitters. But ask any bartender, and they'll tell you its ubiquity does not debase its worth. Hang by a bespoke cocktail bar for a few too many drinks, and you'll fall within earshot of the great debate over what makes for the "perfect Old Fashioned."

The Old Fashioned may be evocative of men in suits, cigars in hand, behind a smoky curtain in the liquor-forbidden Prohibition years, but it's also elegant and raw and primed for experimentation within its classic formula. There is a suggestion hidden within this iconic cocktail to look forward to new perspectives and new flavors. To make the drink your own.

Throughout history, trailblazing women have considered the status quo, and what came before them, and worked to improve it. They contributed to a new narrative, one that was inclusive. One that was not just composed of those men in suits, cigars in hand, and one that didn't allow just a single path to achieve a goal. Follow their lead. Learn how to create a classic, or put your own twist on it, but most important, be yourself and make it your own. And smash the patriarchy while you're at it.

Now take everything you've just learned and everything you thought you knew and SMASH the compulsion to conform! SMASH a sugar cube with some bitters and water! SMASH any preconceptions of a single right way to make this drink! Establish your own belief system within a historical framework that agrees with your principles and your palate—then SMASH it all together in a glass, and stir yourself a damn good cocktail.

MORNING Gloria Steinem

IN A COUPE

1 oz RYe WHISKEY
1 oz BRANDY
¼ oz tRIPLe SEc
¼ oz SIMPLe SYRUP
4 dasHes PeYCHAUD's bitters

· StiR · SeRve Up ·

GLORIA STEINEM

A woman without a man is like a fish without a bicycle.
—Gloria Steinem

With a career that spans decades, Gloria Steinem is undoubtedly one of America's foremost feminist pioneers and visionaries. She has been both a role model and a lightning rod, depending on the fashion and politics of the time, and has inspired countless women with her eloquent lectures, writing, and action.

Steinem gained widespread notoriety in 1963 by going undercover as a "Bunny" to expose the mistreatment of women at Playboy Clubs, but her career in journalism continued throughout the 1960s and onward. She was one of the founders of *New York* magazine, where she wrote a column on politics, penning such pieces as "After Black Power, Women's Liberation," and later helped launch *Ms.* magazine. She said of *Ms.*, "I realized as a journalist that there really was nothing for women to read that was controlled by women," so in January 1972, *Ms.* first hit newsstands, featuring, appropriately, Wonder Woman on the cover.

Steinem has been recognized for her work on behalf of women by the American Civil Liberties Union, the United Nations, and numerous colleges and universities. In 2013, she was awarded the Presidential Medal of Freedom. Her 2015 memoir, *My Life on the Road*, is a toast-worthy testament to a career spent transforming the lives of women around her. Now, as feminism is beginning to experience a renaissance, it only feels right to raise a glass to one of the most influential women's rights activists for her unparalleled contributions to the cause.

This cocktail is meant to be consumed in the morning as a strong antidote to a hangover. So make sure not to Ms. your window. Just kidding; morning, noon, or night, it tastes great. Have a few. . . . Remember, no guts, no Gloria!

eMILY dRINK-iNSON

IN AN OLD FaSHIONeD gLASS

Muddle 4 cRANBERRIES*
& 1 oRANGE SLICE

- 2½ oz bouRBON
- ½ oz MAPLE SYRuP
- 2 daSHES ANGoSTuRA bitteRS

*NO FReSH CRANBERRIES HANDY?
Substitute 2 tbsp
of tART CRANBERRY
SAuCe

Cranberries are Red
Whiskey is Brown
Together they turn
My frown upside down
× E.D.

gARNISH WITH
ROSeMARY SpRIg
&
A CRANBERRY

- HARd SHAKe•
- double STRAIN oveR Ice•
- top WITH A SPLASH of gINGER ALE•

EMILY DICKINSON

EMILY DRINK-INSON (WHISKEY CRANBERRY SMASH)

A word is dead when it is said, some say. I say it just begins to live that day.
                                                    —Emily Dickinson

Emily Dickinson is one of the most beloved and revered American poets in history. Her extensive collection of poetry and personal letters is numbered in the thousands, yet, with the exception of fewer than a dozen published works, her poetry was not celebrated—let alone *discovered*—until after her death at the age of fifty-five.

Dickinson led a private, and later reclusive, life in Amherst, Massachusetts. In contrast to her shy demeanor, Dickinson's poetry is emotional and uninhibited, and it often verges on confessional. Her poems continue to have a powerful influence on the literary world, but they were especially striking in a time when taking risks in prose and poetry was unusual and often frowned upon, particularly for a woman. Her writing challenged the conventional style of verse and grammar and encouraged a sense of poetic freedom. Although she was not a self-proclaimed feminist, Dickinson's work projects a strong early feminist voice and has undoubtedly encouraged many women—and poets in general—to use language to be subversive, imaginative, and adventurous.

Since Dickinson never strayed far from home, the cranberry bogs of Massachusetts would've been a convenient hop, skip, and a jump away to gather the right mixer for this drink. Enjoy it in your room alone and let your pen pals know how delicious this cocktail is. Slap a rosemary sprig on top to brighten it (bonus points if you grow them yourself, as Emily, an avid botanist, would have done). You may feel averse to drinking alone, but after a few of these you'll feel Emily'on times better. I pro-prose a toast: to Emily Dickinson!

WHISKEY Sour-fragettes

IN A HIGHBALL

- 2 oz BOURBON
- 1 oz LEMON JUICE
- 3/4 oz Simple Syrup

GARNISH WITH
LEMON WEDGE
&
A CHERRY

AN OLD-SCHOOL WHISKEY SOUR
is MADE WITH AN egg WHITE.
After You're done egging
the courthouse, toss AN
egg WHITE iN THE MIX! ✓

VOTE
☑ WHISKEY
☐ gin
☐ VODKA
☐ RUM

•SHAKE•
Serve over Ice

WOMEN'S SUFFRAGE

WHISKEY SOUR-FRAGETTES (WHISKEY SOUR)

I never doubted that equal rights was the right direction. Most reforms, most problems are complicated. But to me there is nothing complicated about ordinary equality.

Alice Paul

At the core of democracy is the right to a voice, and a vote is a crucial vehicle to ensure that one's voice is heard. Seems a little hypocritical, then, that for centuries under the supposed democracy in the United States and throughout much of the world, more than half of the population wasn't permitted a voice. In the late 1800s, an international crusade formed against this injustice, as women around the world began to fight for their right to vote.

With the help of pioneering reformers like Susan B. Anthony and Alice Paul, women took to the streets, went on hunger strikes, and risked their lives to demand the same rights that men possessed. After a grueling struggle in the United States, the right to vote came in 1920 with the passage of the Nineteenth Amendment. Elsewhere a similar fight for universal suffrage slowly generated results. Still, in the United States, nearly a century after the Nineteenth amendment was ratified, the process for casting a vote is often made difficult for marginalized communities. Knowing that injustices continue despite the long fight to gain these rights is all the more reason to use your voice, get out there, and vote.

Before casting a vote in favor of the whiskey sour, consider that a "sour" is simply defined as a drink with citrus, sugar, and your chosen spirit. The most common is the Whiskey Sour, but feel free to elect another spirit in its place. Be an informed drinker—it's not just a privilege; it's a duty. Now that's something we can all suffra-get behind!

SYLVIA CARRÉ-VERA

IN A ROCKS GLASS

WAY
SYLVIA RIVERA

BLVD
VIEUX CARRÉ

1 oz RYE WHISKEY

1 oz COGNAC

3/4 oz BÉNÉDICTINE

1 oz SWEET VERMOUTH

1 dASH ANGOSTURA &

1 dASH PeYCHAUD'S bitters

StiR

Serve OveR

SHIMMERING

STONeWALL INN

ROCKS

SYLVIA RIVERA

SYLVIA CARRÉ-VERA (VIEUX CARRÉ)

Hell hath no fury like a drag queen scorned.

—Sylvia Rivera

Hailed as the Rosa Parks of the Transgender Movement, Sylvia Rivera was an outspoken advocate for transgender people and queer youth. Growing up on the streets of New York City in the 1960s as a transgender girl of Puerto Rican and Venezuelan descent, Rivera faced discrimination but never shied away from speaking out against bigotry. At a time when the LGBTQ community was condemned almost unanimously by society, Rivera bravely used her voice, actions, and attention-grabbing persona to illuminate injustices. Alongside close friend and fellow activist Marsha P. Johnson, she founded Street Transvestite Action Revolutionaries (STAR), which gave support to young, homeless, queer, and trans people of color.

Today, the Sylvia Rivera Law Project works to further self-determination and expression of gender identity for all, regardless of income or race. Rivera's refusal to yield to discrimination both catalyzed the inclusion of transgender rights under the umbrella of the larger gay rights movement and has distinguished her as a fearless pioneer and activist.

The Vieux Carré cocktail originated in New Orleans, a city often associated with its fabulous parties, spirit of celebration, and aggrandized aesthetic. But it's also a city that has endured considerable struggle and mistreatment. Certainly no drink is fully capable of celebrating Sylvia Rivera's own displays of grace, optimism, and relentlessness in the face of adversity, but if we're going to choose one it should be this beloved cocktail of the Big Easy. Rivera could Carré the weight of this drink, but after a few, we all may need help standing up, Orleans'ing on one another for support.

OUR BODIES, OURSELVES

OUR TODDIES, OURSELVES (HOT TODDY)

Originally denounced as "pornographic filth" for its honest and comprehensive discussions on women's health, *Our Bodies, Ourselves* is one of the most important and groundbreaking works of literature on this topic to date. First self-published in 1970 by a collective of twelve women, and selling for thirty-five cents a copy, *OBOS* came into being at a time when just 10 percent of the physicians in America were women. The book was instrumental in fighting archaic methods in health care for women, which had up until that point been dictated by condescension, paternalism, sexism, and withholding of information. Decidedly feminist, but not anti-male, *OBOS* grew organically from women sharing the experiences they had with the medical establishment and their doctors, discussing subjects like menstruation, sexual abuse, abortion, masturbation, disease, hygiene, pregnancy and childbirth, menopause, sexuality, sexual health, gender identity, and birth control. The availability of this book offered a shift in possibility, wherein women could view and control their own bodies as autonomous, empowered beings. With a focus on access to information for adolescent girls, *OBOS* also helped coalesce a sense of personal self-governing of one's own body from a young age.

The initial self-printing sold 250,000 copies solely through word of mouth, and in the decades since, the book has sold more than four million copies in thirty languages. The OBOS Global Initiative continues to work with and support women's groups worldwide, aiding in adapting *OBOS* for each distinct culture and community.

This cocktail doesn't only warm you up; it offers soothing and healing ingredients so you can take your health into your own hands. Try drinking this cocktail in front of a mirror and studying yourself closely.

Slouching toward Bethle-Hammered

IN A MASON JAR

- 3/4 oz (1½ tbsp) HONEY (OR MORE TO TASTE)
- ½ oz (1 tbsp) APPLE CIDER VINEGAR
- ½ oz LEMON JUICE
- 1 tsp FRESH GRATED TURMERIC (OR ⅓ tsp DRIED)
- 2 tsp FRESH GRATED GINGER & PINCH OF GROUND PEPPERCORN
- ~ 1 CUP WATER
- 2 OZ BOURBON *

* A CLASSIC SWITCHEL IS MADE WITHOUT BOOZE, BUT THAT'S NO FUN! TRY IT BOTH WAYS.

THE SWITCHEL IS A GREAT HEALTH ELIXIR THAT BOOSTS THE IMMUNE SYSTEM, INCREASES ENERGY, SPEEDS METABOLISM & MAKES YOU A BETTER WRITER. WELL, MOST OF THAT'S TRUE. IN ANY CASE, IT'LL HELP YOU BETHLE-HAMMER OUT YOUR WORK.

- STIR - SERVE OVER ICE -

JOAN DIDION

SLOUCHING TOWARD BETHLE-HAMMERED
(BOURBON SWITCHEL)

We tell ourselves stories in order to live.   —Joan Didion

J oan Didion is an American essayist and novelist with a poet's eye
for the world and a journalist's instinct for precision. With a career spanning more than six decades, her works demonstrate diverse creativity in content, form, and style. Her best-known work,
Slouching Towards Bethlehem, published in 1968, collected previously
published pieces that fell under the freshly minted term "New Journalism." *Slouching* opens with a series of essays written as observation
and testament to mid-sixties California. The title piece, in particular,
describes a San Francisco grounded more in hard reality and less in
the mythic, utopian images usually found; a world that spoke to Didion as one of disorder and anxiety yet still awash in California sunshine. In the essay "On Keeping a Notebook," she sips whiskey while
chomping on sauerkraut, tickling the readers' senses as she explores
the importance of recording and remembering.

Among Didion's later literary works is *The Year of Magical Thinking*,
written as a way to tunnel through the grief of losing her husband
and the serious illness faced by her daughter. Hailed as a classic book
about mourning, it went on to win the National Book Award in 2005.
Didion's mastery and eloquence in illustrating the human condition
in a modern American landscape solidify her as one of the most important and iconic authors of her generation.

*Got writer's block? Holed up in your room until your deadline? The Switchel
is the perfect health elixir that, paired with whiskey, will keep your mind
and body on its A game. Don't risk missing a deadline or interrupting work
flow—it's easy to batch, by doubling, tripling, or quadrupling the recipe.
Didion't anyone tell you? The words will flow right out of you once you've
made a dent in that jar.*

EMMA GOLD·MANHATTAN
IN A CHILLED COUPE

2 oz RYe WHISKEY

1 oz Sweet VeRMOUTH

2 dAsHes Angostura bitters

GARNiSH WiTH A golden cherry

How to make the best MANHATTAN:
eXcHANge ingredients using
Self-provisioning barter systems,
collectively organize, build A free
SpAce with SHARed ideas &
Responsibilities, Renounce capitalism
SAMPLe, SHARe, RePeAt

· StiR · Serve Up ·

EMMA GOLDMAN

EMMA GOLD-MANHATTAN (MANHATTAN)

If I can't dance, I don't want to be part of your revolution.
—Emma Goldman

Emma Goldman was one of the most influential activists associated with anarchist philosophy and early women's rights. She spent her life examining concepts of power, freedom, sexuality, militarism, prisons, homosexuality, and religion in an attempt to envision an alternative society. Anarchism is often portrayed as a system that breeds chaos, destruction, and violent revolution; however, Goldman's work advocated for a society that relied on voluntary cooperation and the exposing of what she believed to be a violent and corrupt "false" democracy. Much of her work, including her seminal autobiography *Living My Life*, championed the belief that hierarchichal government and patriarchy created oppressive structures that prohibited the practice of free thought. Goldman was persecuted and imprisoned numerous times for her activism, but that never stopped her from sharing her opinions, no matter how controversial. She was a committed revolutionary, even regarded by the press as "the most dangerous woman in America" and a "rebel woman"—rebellious because she was a freethinking advocate for equal rights, and dangerous because she believed the revolution was inevitable. After her death in 1940, much of her work faded into obscurity; it wasn't until the 1970s feminist movement that she again became lionized as a revolutionary thinker and feminist.

Em-matters not if you prefer the Manhattan served up or on the rocks, only that you drink it with conviction. After you taste it, you'll want to get out there and dance. Don't worry if you lack rhythm; at least you've got a heart of Goldman. The revolution starts with you! And whiskey!

TO: ♀❀ ALL GIRLS ♀ ❀
Bikini Kill, Le Tigre, Sleater-Kinney, Bratmobile
L7, Red Aunts, Heavens to Betsy...
Babes in Toyland

Rock

'N'
RYe-ot gRRRL

IN AN OLD FASHIONED GLASS

- ○ 2oz RYe WHISKEY
- ◇ HANDFUL of POP ROCKS
    OR OTHER ROCK CANDY
- ◇ gARNISH WITH WHATEVER THE f*cK
    YOU WANT!

- ○ SeRVE OVER cRUSHED ICE &
    SMASHED PATRIARCHY!

RIOT GRRRLS

ROCK 'N' RYE-OT GRRRL (ROCK & RYE)

I didn't just hit the glass ceiling, I pressed my naked [breasts]
up against it.   —Kathleen Hanna

The Riot Grrrl Movement grew out of the punk and indie rock scene of the Pacific Northwest in the 1990s. Bands like Bikini Kill, Bratmobile, and Sleater-Kinney epitomized the sound and ethos of young women who, sick of sexism and harassment, took control of their scene. They began storming the stage to express themselves without restriction, the same way their male counterparts in punk always had.

Fueled by equal parts rage and empowerment, the movement embraced a combination of third-wave feminism and punk rock politics, championing diversity of thought, race, sexuality, gender expression, and appearance. Kathleen Hanna of Bikini Kill said it straight in the "Riot Grrrl Manifesto":

"BECAUSE us girls crave records and books and fanzines that speak to US that WE feel included in and can understand in our own ways . . .

"BECAUSE we are angry at a society that tells us Girl = Dumb, Girl = Bad, Girl = Weak . . .

"BECAUSE I believe with my wholeheartmindbody that girls constitute a revolutionary soul force that can, and will change the world for real."

Powered by zines, punk rock venues, and the bands leading the DIY charge, the Riot Grrrl Movement inspired young women everywhere to stand up for themselves, smash the patriarchy, and have fun doing it.

What's the urban legend about Pop Rocks and whiskey? Mix them together and you start a Rrrrevolution? You cand-deny that sounds good. Up the puns!

Simone de Boulevardier

in an old fashioned glass

1½ oz Bourbon

¾ oz Sweet Vermouth

¾ oz Campari

> For a French twist, substitute a cognac for the bourbon. Drink outside the box.

Garnish with mandarin orange twist

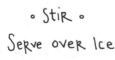

∘ Stir ∘
Serve over Ice

SIMONE DE BEAUVOIR

SIMONE DE BOULEVARDIER (BOULEVARDIER)

One is not born, but rather becomes, a woman.
—Simone de Beauvoir, *The Second Sex*

Revered for her writing and philosophical thinking, Simone de Beauvoir had an impressive body of work. In 1954, she won the Prix Goncourt, awarded to the best and most imaginative prose work of the year, for her book *The Mandarins*. She was perhaps best known, however, as a founder of modern feminist thought via her landmark work *The Second Sex*. Published in 1949, the book was met with great resistance and controversy. Critics called it pornography and refused to acknowledge it as credible social theory. The Vatican even went so far as to place it on its list of forbidden texts. Within the thousand-page book, de Beauvoir examined the role of women in the world and the consequences of existence in opposition to men, who take the central (or defining) role within human history. De Beauvoir built the case for women to step out of this diminished essence and become wholly realized on their own, defined by no one but themselves.

De Beauvoir lived the life she wrote about, a life that resisted traditional definitions of womanhood. Amid growing postwar social reforms, her work rejected patriarchal limitations and helped inspire early second-wave feminism. Don't you think she'd be a great cocktail-party guest? *Oui oui!* I agree!

De Beauvoir was a thinker on every level, so naturally this French take on the classic Negroni is a no-brainer. Have one, have two, then have Simo're. Challenge your senses and unlock that Second Sex'tion of your psyche to explore some great ideas and to really get the most out of your drunken rendezvous.

Civil Rye'ts
move-mint Julep

ditch the old fashioned glass
serve in a hurricane glass

◊ muddle 4 mint leaves & 1 sugar cube

◊ 2 oz Rye whiskey
◊ mint garnish

• stir things up •

• serve •
over crushed ice

THE CIVIL RIGHTS MOVEMENT

CIVIL RYE'TS MOVE-MINT JULEP (MINT JULEP)

The Civil Rights Movement sought to bring the equal rights promised under the Constitution to African Americans and other marginalized groups. The 1954 Supreme Court decision *Brown v. Board of Education of Topeka* ended the practice of "separate but equal" schools (at least on paper) and is often considered the beginning of the movement. Dedicated nonviolent protests, such as the Montgomery bus boycott and the Greensboro, North Carolina sit-ins, continued to bring inequalities to light.

On August 28, 1963, 250,000 people gathered in front of the Lincoln Memorial to peacefully protest and support the civil rights legislation proposed by President John F. Kennedy. The event closed with Dr. Martin Luther King Jr.'s timeless "I Have a Dream" speech. The following year, the Civil Rights Act of 1964 was signed, banning discrimination based on "race, color, religion, sex or national origin" in employment practices and public accommodations. The bill allowed the attorney general to file lawsuits for enforcement, nullifying state and local laws supporting discrimination.

The Civil Rights Movement would not have been successful without strong women like Rosa Parks, Ella Baker, Daisy Bates, Fannie Lou Hamer, Dorothy Height, Diane Nash, Septima Poinsette Clark, and Jo Ann Robinson fighting for structural and systemic change. The African American Civil Rights Movement led to a radical shift in the perception of human rights as a whole, reconstituting beliefs about one person being inferior to another—black or white, man or woman—and the imperative to dismantle these structures of oppression.

It's time for the Julep to get a makeover—the cocktail is the very embodiment of the upper-class white South. Along with the ice, crush that narrowed view and serve this delicious drink to all. It'll be the crown jul' of your party.

ZORA (RUSTY) NEALE
tHiRST - ON

IN AN OLD FASHIONED GLASS

2 oz BLENDED ScotcH

3/4 oz DRAMbuie

SpLASH WITH WATER ... to QuENCH
YOUR tHiRST

∘ ServE OVER ONE LARGE RocK ∘

ZORA NEALE HURSTON

ZORA (RUSTY) NEALE THIRST-ON (RUSTY NAIL)

Some people could look at a mud puddle and see an ocean with ships.

—Zora Neale Hurston

Writer and anthropologist Zora Neale Hurston was a central figure during the Harlem Renaissance, recognized for her storytelling and unique observations on the world. In the 1920s, she began her writing career in earnest, linking her fiction with a passion for African American folklore. Her return to her home-town in Florida led to the 1935 publication of *Mules and Men*, a collection of short stories, fables, and songs that gave voice to authentic southern black storytellers.

The 1930s and '40s saw Hurston's rise to prominence. Her best-received work, *Their Eyes Were Watching God*, was published in 1937. Despite her success, Hurston faded into obscurity until Alice Walker called attention to her powerful feminist nature in 1977, when Walker wrote, "I became aware of my need of Zora Neale Hurston's work some time before I knew her work existed." Hurston's elegant prose created a landscape for a larger shared experience—especially for many black readers—as she dared to be authentic in her writing and in her life.

The Rusty Nail, a cocktail that similarly faded into a momentary obscurity, is still as powerful as ever. It is imaginative and bold and timeless and never Zor-ing. Like holy water, it will quench your thirst and, before you know it, you'll be staring into the sky—your eyes watching God (or, rather, whoever or whatever floats your boat in the mud puddle of life).

Blood & S'antigone

IN AN OLD FASHIONED GLASS

1½ oz Scotch

½ oz Sweet Vermouth

½ oz Cherry Heering

½ oz Lemon Juice

GARNISH WITH
Blood Orange Wedge

• SHAKE • Serve over Ice •

ANTIGONE

BLOOD & S'ANTIGONE (BLOOD & SAND)

Leave me to my own absurdity.   —Sophocles, *Antigone*

W ritten around 441 BC by the Greek playwright Sophocles, *Antigone* is a tragedy, featuring one of the original heroines and martyrs of literature. In it, the headstrong Antigone refuses to submit to her uncle Creon, the tyrant King of Thebes, when he bans her from burying her brother, Polynices. Antigone defies his orders, and when Creon finds out, he imprisons Antigone in a tomb where she is to be starved to death. Eventually her uncle has a change of heart, but it's too late—Antigone has hanged herself. Her death prompts a wave of suicides, including that of Creon's son and wife. Creon finds himself alone on his throne, devastated by the consequences caused by his own pride.

Through the lens of complex characters like Antigone, Sophocles confronts readers with the enduring philosophical inquiries into human consciousness: empathy, love, power, fate, morality, and mortality. Antigone's actions remind readers of the dangers of totalitarianism and the importance of self-determination. She never wavered in her commitment, solidly sticking to the principles of free will. Although she met a tragic demise, Antigone embodies the ultimate female warrior.

A big dose of integrity, a splash of loyalty, a hefty pinch of courage, a few dashes of sacrifice and defiance, toss in some stubbornness for balance and good measure, and you've got a full-fledged heroine who really knows how to stir things up. Make this cocktail at your next party; it'll be a bloody hit.

I AM WOMAN, HEAR ME ROY!

IN A CHILLED COUPE

- 2 oz Scotch
- 1 oz Sweet Vermouth
- 2 dashes Angostura bitters
  - 2 dashes Orange bitters

CHERRY GARNISH

• Stir • Serve Up •

I AM WOMAN, HEAR ME ROAR!

I AM WOMAN, HEAR ME ROY! (ROB ROY)

An anthem for the rising feminist movement of the 1970s, "I am Woman" was an international sensation thanks to its powerful message. Written by Helen Reddy in 1971, the song is not an angry protest cry but a celebration of strength. The song was released at a time when standing up and demanding equal pay in the workplace, representation in government, and fair reproductive rights was often met with disheartening opposition, and it quickly became the soundtrack that women needed to remind themselves of their fight. It's a celebratory anthem for sure, but it's also a reminder that despite the pain and struggle, we *have* in the past, we *can* presently, and we *will* continue to endure. And it's pretty damn catchy to boot. The fact that it was at the top of the Billboard Hot 100 charts for multiple weeks during that era was revolutionary in and of itself.

Legend holds that at the National Organization for Women's 1973 annual convention gala, the evening closed with "I Am Woman," and within a few moments the entire room was engaged—hundreds of women holding hands, dancing, and singing along. It's difficult to say if this song fueled a movement, but it *definitely* fueled one or two rowdy, drunken sing-alongs.

A take on the iconic Manhattan, a Rob Roy uses the more conventionally "masculine" scotch as its base spirit. Well, listen up! If you think you can Rob half the population of one of the most beautifully complex spirits in existence because it's more fit for a man, you are Roy-ally mistaken, sir! Roar not getting off scotch-free this time. Move over, "manly" drink; this one's for everyone. If you can't hear that, Roar not listening.

take
Pickle-back the Night
in two shot glasses

☆ in the first ☆

◖ 1½ oz moonshine whiskey

(Don't waste the good stuff. You're
not drinking it for the taste.)

☆ in the second ☆

◖ 1½ oz briny pickle juice

◖ top with pepper spray
(or a pinch of black pepper)

then in quick
succession

take 'em back

TAKE BACK THE NIGHT

TAKE PICKLE-BACK THE NIGHT (MOONSHINE PICKLEBACK)

This international campaign was set into motion in the early 1970s, after several violent acts committed against women walking home alone at night were largely ignored. This, compounded with other discriminatory activities of the time, incited rallies, marches, candlelight vigils, and direct action initiatives around Europe and North America. It has since spread to more than thirty countries and spurred the development of numerous organizations, support groups, and awareness campaigns seeking to end all forms of sexual violence and assault and create safer streets and communities. Take Back the Night marches and rallies are held annually in cities around the world and continue to urge safer streets and increase awareness of the continued violence against women—so that we can take back the night for the nocturnal pleasures and celebrations that it's meant for.

This drink will send you over the moon, and not just 'cause it's so boozy. Feel free to drink this at night, or during the day, or whenever you feel like it. It may pickle your liver, but at least your friends will be there to walk you home if you've had one too many.

GIN

DOLLY PARTON MY FRENCH 75

IN A flute
OR A boot

- 1 oz gin
- ½ oz Lemon Juice
- ½ oz Simple Syrup
- top with dry Sparkling wine

garnish with Lemon twist

♫ workin' wine to 5 —
what a way to make
a livin' ♫

DOLLY PARTON

DOLLY PARTON MY FRENCH 75 (FRENCH 75)

If you don't like the road you're walking, start paving another one.
                                                    —Dolly Parton

Mega-icon, music entertainer, sex symbol, feminist, American darling, businesswoman, and role model Dolly Parton has garnered superstardom by carving out a career that is as unique and fabulous as she is. After being named the Female Vocalist of the Year by the Country Music Association in 1975, she rose to broader pop-culture prominence by starring in the film *9 to 5*. Her recording of the title track reached number one on pop and country charts and earned her an Academy Award nomination for Best Original Song; soon after, she starred in the film *The Best Little Whorehouse in Texas*, further solidifying her as one of the most powerful female performers of the era. Her success reached a peak with the launch of the Dollywood amusement park, where, you guessed it—it's all Dolly everything.

Behind the big hair, fringed plunging neckline, and bedazzled cowboy boots, Parton has also created a philanthropic legacy through her generous support of many causes, from HIV/AIDS-related charities to childhood literacy. In 2005, she was given the National Medal of Arts, and in 2006, she received Kennedy Center Honors for her lifetime contribution to the arts. As a woman in the public eye as well as a performer, Parton has found a way to harness her sexuality and talent through a tongue-in-cheek exploitation of it. Forget 9 to 5; Parton's legacy is working 24/7.

Try adding a lemon peel and serve this drink at the zest little whorehouse in Texas or in your home—whichever is easier. To get the full effect, try a cheap Champagne, Dolly up your hair so it's taller than the Eiffel Tower, and Jo-lean on your friends.

MALA-Lillet

IN A COUPE

- 1½ oz gin
- ½ oz vodka
- ¼ oz Lillet

Garnish with thyme sprig

• Stir • Serve up •

MALALA YOUSAFZAI

MALA-LILLET (VESPER)

We realize the importance of our voices only when we are silenced.

—Malala Yousafzai

Born and raised in the Swat Valley area of Pakistan, Malala Yousafzai began speaking out against the Taliban's attacks on girls' schools as a teenager in 2008, with a speech entitled "How Dare the Taliban Take Away My Basic Right to Education." News of the speech spread, and Malala's activism soon brought her worldwide acclaim. In 2011, she was nominated for the International Children's Peace Prize and awarded Pakistan's National Youth Peace Prize.

The Taliban was angered by this attention and issued a death threat against Malala. In October 2012, fifteen-year-old Malala was shot in the head on her way to school and critically wounded by a masked gunman. Miraculously, she survived, and on her sixteenth birthday she spoke at the United Nations as a living symbol against violence. In 2014, she became the youngest recipient of the Nobel Peace Prize.

No one could have expected the power of one girl's voice to galvanize a cause, but by attempting to silence her, the Taliban amplified her message into one heard around the world. Her eloquence and compassion—always speaking with hope instead of anger, despite the horrors she has witnessed and endured—are truly inspiring. Malala's words and her work through the Malala Fund continue to support the education and freedom of girls everywhere.

Malala is below the legal drinking age, it's true, but we can all enjoy a second serving of this cocktail in her honor. Learn this recipe, and then teach it to others. Malala'f your friends will be singing your praises, Lillet into the night—even if it's well past your bedtime.

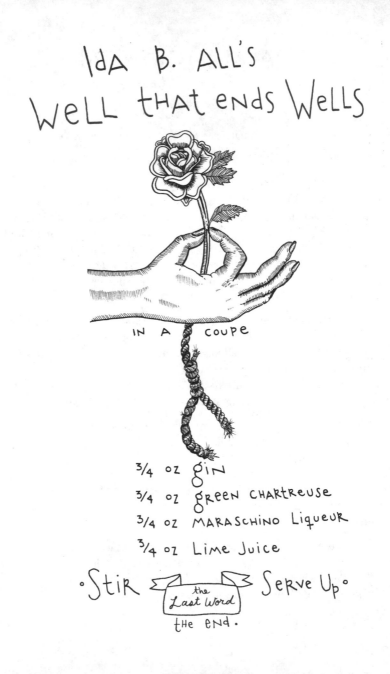

IdA B. ALL'S
WeLL tHAt eNds WeLLs

IN A COUPE

3/4 oz gin

3/4 oz green CHARtReUSe

3/4 oz MARASCHINO LiqueuR

3/4 oz Lime Juice

•Stir — the Last Word — Serve Up•

tHe eNd.

IDA B. WELLS

> *The people must know before they can act, and there is no educator to compare with the press.*
>
> —Ida B. Wells

B orn a slave a few months before the Emancipation Proclamation, Ida B. Wells was a journalist, activist, feminist, and suffragist who fought against the injustices of the post-Reconstruction era. After a white mob lynched a friend of Wells's, she urged the black population to move away from Memphis, as the city did nothing to protect their life or property. More than six thousand heeded her words and fled, while others took up a boycott of white-owned businesses. In 1892, Wells began an anti-lynching campaign with the pamphlet "Southern Horrors: Lynch Law in All Its Phases," and three years later, she published a follow-up, "The Red Record," which cataloged the crimes and acts of violence that had been perpetrated against black Americans since the end of the Civil War. Wells founded the National Association of Colored Women's Clubs in 1896 and was one of the founding members of the National Association for the Advancement of Colored People (NAACP).

Although her work caught the attention of white northerners, it did little, if anything, to change the minds of white southerners at the time. But it still created ripples; her outrage did not fall on deaf ears, and many rose up and joined her cause. Her brave crusade for justice in the face of tyranny and terror remains a beacon to political activists.

The Last Word cocktail is fitting to pay tribute to this badass woman. Ida B. crazy not to say she deserves the last word on this one. Try opting for a step up from your bottom-of-the-barrel Well(s) liquor and use a top-shelf London Dry to raise your glass to this courageous crusader. No garnish necessary; the drink speaks for itself. The end.

Debbie
HAIR of the dog

IN A CHILLED ROCKS GLASS
WITH LIPSTICK TRACES

3/4 oz Gin

3/4 oz triple Sec

3/4 oz Lillet blANC

3/4 oz Lemon Juice

dASH of AbsintHe
(OR AbsintHe RiNse)

GARNiSH WitH
BRiGHt-YELLOW Lemon twist

ONE WAY OR ANOTHER, I'M gONNA
GEt YA, GEt YA, GEt YA, GEt YA ... dRUNK!

° SHAKE • Serve Up (tHe PUNKS!) °

DEBBIE HARRY

DEBBIE HAIR OF THE DOG (CORPSE REVIVER #2)

The only person I really believe in is me.   —Debbie Harry

As one of the most recognizable icons of the 1970s New York punk scene, Debbie Harry undoubtedly paved the way for women in punk rock. With her signature bleach-blonde fringe and lyrics about sexuality and desire, Harry was a punk anomaly, taking the blonde-bombshell stereotype and turning it on its head. She and guitarist Chris Stein formed Blondie in 1974, and the band quickly became regular performers at New York punk institutions like CBGB's and Max's Kansas City. The band found critical and commercial success with their third album, 1978's *Parallel Lines*, which sold more than twenty million copies worldwide and featured their megahit "Heart of Glass." Harry herself soon became synonymous with Blondie the band, prompting the group to mass-produce "Blondie is a Group!" buttons in 1979. But even with the distinction made, Harry unquestionably embodied the band's powerful, stylish, anti-authoritarian spirit. Blondie achieved a sound that penetrated cultural consciousness and found a raw space of convergence between mainstream pop culture, exploitative social constructs, and the absurd. The band went on to record several more albums and continued their airwave dominance with memorable songs like "One Way or Another," "Hanging on the Telephone," and "Call Me"; their eleventh album, *Pollinator*, was released in 2017. Blondie was inducted into the Rock & Roll Hall of Fame in 2006, but Harry deserves special recognition as a talented and fierce pioneer of women in rock.

For an authentic hair of the dog experience, wake up, chug whatever flat beer was left next to your bed, hope that it's free of cigarette butts, then proceed to your cocktail. You'd CBG-Be as good as dead before letting your hangover win, so drink up or shut up! Blondeep breaths, you'll be revived back from the Deb in no time!

Bijou-dy Chicago

IN A COUPE

- 1 oz gin
- 1 oz green chartreuse
- 1 oz sweet vermouth

2 dashes orange bitters

garnish with edible flower
(try nasturtium or honeysuckle)

· Stir · Serve Up ·

JUDY CHICAGO

BIJOU-DY CHICAGO (BIJOU)

J udy Chicago is a prominent American artist from the second-wave feminist movement of the 1970s. Her defining work, *The Dinner Party*, created in 1979, was a tribute to some of the most influential women—mythical and real—throughout history. Using ceramic sculpture as "kitchen china," she created individual place settings for thirty-nine women around a giant, triangular table. On a floor made of porcelain tiles were the names of many more women, 999 in total. The shape and mere scale of *The Dinner Party* were an embodiment of women and strength—not to mention the perhaps more obvious symbolism that each unique dinner plate unmistakably resembled female genitalia. This iconic work was unsurprisingly met with disapproval from the male-dominated art world, but it was also criticized from within the feminist movement. For some, her work was beloved for its tribute to women and its daring attempt to display the female form in a new way, but for many others, it was an added example of women being reduced to objects of consumption, fertility, bondage, and sex. Regardless of your critiques of *The Dinner Party*, or Chicago's entire body of work, it's undeniable that she's essential to the feminist movement of the 1970s, both as a social critic as well as a gifted fine artist and sculptor. . . . She's certainly worth pulling up a chair for—even if you never make it past the hors d'oeuvres.

Try this cocktail as a meal accompaniment, if you'd like. Or as an aperitif. Or why not skip dinner altogether and just make a meal of it? It will definitely satisfy your hunger. I Judy'clare, this drink is refreshing!

MAe-VIATION JEMISON

IN A COCKTAIL GLASS

- 2 oz gin
- $\frac{1}{2}$ oz MARASCHINO LIQUEUR
- $\frac{1}{4}$ oz CRÈME de VIOLETTE
- 1 oz LEMON JUICE

✦ PAIRS WELL WITH A MARS BAR OR MILKY WAY ✦

◦ SHAKE ◦
SERVE UP. (OR ON THE ROCKETS.)

MAE JEMISON

MAE-VIATION JEMISON (AVIATION)

Never be limited by other people's limited imaginations. If you adopt their attitudes, then the possibility won't exist because you'll have already shut it out. . . . You can hear other people's wisdom, but you've got to re-evaluate the world for yourself.

—Mae Jemison

On September 12, 1992, Mae Jemison became the first African American woman in space, breaking a barrier . . . as well as the pull of gravity. From a young age, she knew what she wanted to do, even when her goal flew in the face of gendered expectation. When asked what she wanted to be in kindergarten, she replied, "Scientist." She got "Don't you mean nurse?" in return from her teacher. This only helped further inspire her to live out her dreams.

After earning a medical degree from Cornell Medical College, Jemison joined the Peace Corps, where she faced challenges that toughened her mental resolve and prepared her for the hardships involved with the astronaut program. Once she officially joined NASA in 1987, she was initially discouraged by the lack of female astronauts in the program but remained steadfast and took initiative—she even joked that she may as well try the astronaut route rather than hanging out "in a cornfield, waiting for ET to pick [her] up." Jemison knew the challenges in her career as well as the obstacles of being a black woman in a white male–dominated field, but she reached for the stars nonetheless. Since leaving the space program, Jemison has pursued a career in teaching and developing technology businesses. Her career and accomplishments are simply out of this world.

The Mae-viation will go over great at your next get-together. If the gravity of party planning becomes too overwhelming, don't worry. Take a second, give it some space, and in no time, all that pressure will feel light-years away.

Sloe gin-der equality
†

in an old fashioned glass

(equal parts)

- 3/4 oz London dry gin
- 3/4 oz Sloe gin
- 3/4 oz Campari
- 3/4 oz Sweet vermouth
- Garnish with orange twist
- Stir
- Strain over ice

> It's negronly a matter of time

GENDER EQUALITY

SLOE GIN-DER EQUALITY (NEGRONI)

"I am no bird; and no net ensnares me: I am a free human being with an independent will."

—Charlotte Brontë, *Jane Eyre*

For this cocktail, we're drinking to the belief that all people are entitled to equal rights and opportunities regardless of their gender expression. This issue is complex, for sure, but ultimately, gender equality is an ongoing effort to dismantle centuries of unfair practices put in place by a patriarchal system—a societal structure built on the foundational belief that one group (namely, men) holds the power over another (you guessed it, women).

Many countries have taken initiatives to eliminate the gender pay gap, but there's only so much a law can do to change perceptions of "worth." When you compare equal pay for equal work to equal pay for work of equal value, it gets murky. Even with enforced laws, there's still an imbalance. In the United States today, women still earn only about seventy-nine cents to the dollar of men.

Sure, there are countless subfactions of gender inequality, but just opening up the conversation about gender (a problematic binary in and of itself) can help us strategize ways to unite people rather than divide. Maybe adding sloe gin to the classic Negroni is an homage to the slow and arduous process of achieving these goals and the incremental steps that it takes. Or maybe it's just a super-boozy cocktail that I think we can all agree is damn delicious.

Nothing Camparis to the original, so if you want to enjoy a classic Negroni, just omit the sloe gin from your recipe and mix equal parts (1 ounce each) of the other three ingredients. The key here is equality. Now go on, have another; you Negroni live once.

TOM KALI'NS

IN A COLLINS GLASS

2 oz gin
1 oz Lemon Juice
1 oz Simple Syrup

HANDFUL BLUEBERRIES

GARNISH WITH
Lemon Wedge

○ SHAKE HARD WITH BERRIES • "DIRTY POUR" ALL
ice & berries   ○   top WITH SODA WATER

KALI

TOM KALI'NS (TOM COLLINS)

The Hindu goddess Kali embodies violence, darkness, and sexuality, all while projecting a strong maternal presence. In India, where Hinduism is the predominant religion, Kali is the Dark Mother Goddess among the 330 million gods and goddesses who are worshipped. Perhaps the wildest of all the Hindu deities, Kali is both feared and revered. Legend has it that billions of years ago, when Kali was on a killing spree, her husband, Lord Shiva, stepped in her path. In defiance, she stuck out her long tongue disdainfully, which is how she is depicted in imagery. Generally shown wearing a skirt adorned with severed arms and a necklace of heads and skulls, Kali wears her spoils like trophies. Or like a very extreme fashion statement. Either way, you can pull off anything when your skin is bright blue and you're spattered in blood like Kali is. If you don't mess with this one, she'll protect you and guard you from darkness. Kali, also known as "She who is death," is not represented as an antagonistic deity or as the evil antithesis to life but as an important goddess who reminds people of mortality: that death, along with birth, is the most significant part of life. Plus, could there be a more badass nickname than that?

Need a hand making this drink? Call our girl; she may have a few to spare. Maybe she'll even toss you a whole severed arm! Stick out your tongue, sample the drink, chug it down. It's just to die for. After a few you can Kali't a day! Then do it all again Tom-morrow!

Ursula K. Le Gimlet

in a chilled coupe

2 oz   Gin (or Vodka)

1 oz   Lime Juice

3/4 oz   Simple Syrup

° Shake · Serve Up °

In **The Left Hand of Darkness**, blood is ritualistically mixed into the cement of the stone bridges. To honor this tradition, freeze an ice cube with pomegranate juice in advance & drop into your finished drink.

URSULA K. LE GUIN

URSULA K. LE GIMLET (GIMLET)

The artist deals in what cannot be said in words. The artist whose medium is fiction does this in words. The novelist says in words what cannot be said in words.

—Ursula K. Le Guin

The influential American author Ursula K. Le Guin has written dozens of novels, children's books, short stories, screenplays, and poetry compilations, and is considered one of the most influential science fiction and fantasy writers of the twentieth century. Her work transcends the traditional tropes of science fiction to examine themes like gender, sexuality, anarchism, spirituality, and environmentalism, redefining and transforming the genre in the process and situating herself as a unique feminist voice within a highly male-dominated industry.

Le Guin's work has given authors permission to imaginatively and intellectually combine the real with the surreal in their prose. She is a champion of harnessing the imagination and its raw power to energize and shake people out of the lethargy of daily routine. She offers a port-hole into an imaginative universe that's timeless yet evolving, hopeful even in dystopic domains. Le Guin's writing has helped give a new voice to the science fiction genre as well as inspired new paths for writers in her challenging of ideas of gender and feminism, previously largely unexplored—even, ironically, in worlds based in fantasy where exploration is, in essence, limitless.

Ursula K. Le Guin's writing gim-lets you feel lime you're part of a different world. Maybe you like this world or maybe its hints of the fantastical unnerve you, but either way, it's one worth exploring. To honor one of her most celebrated novels, The Left Hand of Darkness, *try preparing this cocktail with your left hand only. In the dark. Who knows, maybe it will open up an entirely new Univer-sula. (Or maybe it'll just make a mess.)*

ROSA LUXARDO-BURG

IN A CHILLED COUPE

1 1/2 oz Gin (Recommend Old Tom)

1/2 oz Mezcal

1/2 oz Maraschino Liqueur (Luxardo)

3/4 oz Lemon Juice

Garnish with Lemon Twist & A Rose Petal

∘ Stir   Serve Up ∘

ROSA LUXEMBURG

ROSA LUXARDO-BURG (DECEPTION)

> *The masses are the decisive element, they are the rock on which*
> *the final victory of the revolution will be built.*
>
> —Rosa Luxemburg

Rosa Luxemburg was a Marxist theorist, antiwar activist, and revolutionary socialist living in post–World War I Germany. Her 1906 book, *The Mass Strike, the Political Party and the Trade Unions*, promoted the mass strike as a vital tool of the proletariat for attaining socialist victory. The mass strike, she said, had the power to radicalize workers and drive the revolution forward.

Luxemburg split from Germany's Social Democratic Party at the beginning of World War I and helped found the Spartacus League, which aimed to install a new proletarian government and end the war through revolution. After the war, she continued her work agitating against the government, which blamed her for armed clashes in Berlin. The press named her "Bloody Rosa" for these activities, but she did not back down from her fight for workers' rights. In 1919, her actions helped spawn the Spartacist Revolt, which ultimately led to her murder at the hands of the Free Corps, a conservative paramilitary group, making her a martyr to the cause of socialism.

Marx my words, this cocktail is so tasty, workers will strike down your door to request fair self-unionizing and governing institutions where this drink can be collectively prepared, traded, and consumed. You'll be shaking hands and telling everyone that there Gladi-ain't no party like a Spartacus League party. It's going to prole-tear down the house!

Hooli-gin tux-Sparrow

IN A COUPE

- 2 oz gin

- 1 oz DRY fino SHERRY

- 2 dashes orange bitters

GARNISH WITH

A CHERRY SKEWERED ONTO
A MANDARIN ORANGE wedge

• STiR • SERVE Up •

YE HAIYAN (AKA "HOOLIGAN SPARROW")

HOOLI-GIN TUX-SPARROW (TUXEDO)

I have a tough personality. They can't stop me by arresting me or even killing me. —Ye Haiyan

While working at a massage parlor in southern China in the early 2000s, Ye Haiyan, using the pseudonym "Hooligan Sparrow," began a blog documenting her experiences, highlighting the mistreatment of sex workers. It quickly went viral and propelled her on a path to activism. Over the years, Haiyan has become an advocate for sex workers and children and has expressed her beliefs through a variety of highly public and purposefully outrageous acts of protest. In one instance, to expose the deplorable working conditions in brothels, Ye Haiyan advertised "free sex," inciting a media shock wave. Later, seeking justice for six young girls who were abducted and abused by their principal in southern China, Ye Haiyan demonstrated outside the school, holding a sign that read: "Hey, Principal: get a room with me and leave the pupils alone!" After the image circulated and the scandal was met with an international outcry, she faced police and government intimidation. In exposing these human rights violations, her actions helped reveal corrupt surveillance practices and secret policing throughout China but also made her a greater target in the process.

A fearless protector of women and children's rights, Hooligan Sparrow continues to advocate and agitate despite threats against her. She, like the sparrow, is a protector, a creative nest builder, and an expert in camouflage when she needs it, but chiefly, she is a master of flight that demands to be heard when her song is sung.

Try writing this recipe on a big sign and walking the streets telling people how delicious it is. They may ask why, but tell them you'll Sparrow'm the details. Hopefully the message won't fly over their heads.

gin-cess LeiA fizz

IN A COLLINS glass

1½ oz Aperol

1 oz NAVY-Strength gin

¾ oz Lemon Juice

½ oz Honey Syrup

2 dashes Peychaud's / 1 dash Angostura bitters

1 egg white

dRy SHAKE first, then Shake with ice

Pour ~ 1 oz soda water into an empty Collins glass & Pour Contents of Cocktail over the Soda

garnish with Lemon twist

A woman's place is in the Refizz-stance

PRINCESS LEIA

GIN-CESS LEIA FIZZ (GIN FIZZ)

Someone has to save our skins. Into the garbage chute, Flyboy.
—Princess Leia Organa

In the *Star Wars* universe, there is one hero who stands above the rest: Princess (and later General) Leia Organa. If Leia didn't like the situation at hand, she took charge and did what was necessary to improve it. Captured by Darth Vader? She didn't back down; rather, she called him out for being a dog on a leash. Trapped under enemy fire with her crew? It was Leia who grabbed a blaster and made a hole to escape. Forced into bondage and a gold bikini by the literal personification of the slug-minded patriarchy? Leia choked that fool with his own chain.

In 2017, after the death of the inimitable Carrie Fisher, the actress who brought her to life on-screen, Leia was reincarnated as the face of protest. Featured on signs bearing the slogan "A woman's place is in the resistance," or as a mashup with Rosie the Riveter, Leia represents feminine strength against the ugliest oppressions. As a princess, Leia showed us you don't have to wait to be rescued. As a general, she showed us that women can lead the resistance. And, sure, if you want, you can marry a scoundrel and have a family, too. But you don't have to.

Honey, Aperol is said and done, this drink may get you wasted. If someone doesn't want to join you for another round, kindly let them know that they're a stuck-up, half-witted, scruffy-looking nerfherder, and their place is in the resistance (and at the bar) with you. Now tie your hair up in a couple of buns, throw back another fizz, and rebel in the beauty of the night sky. (Is that the moon? Am I seeing double? Triple? How many of these things have I had?)

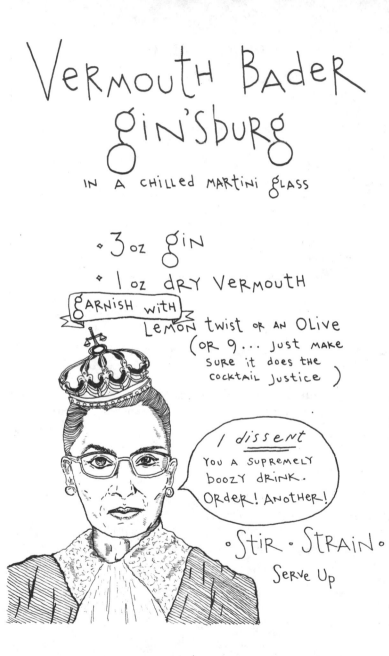

RUTH BADER GINSBURG

VERMOUTH BADER GIN'SBURG (MARTINI)

*People ask me sometimes . . . When do you think there will be
enough women on the court? And my answer is when there are
nine.*   —Ruth Bader Ginsburg

Born in Brooklyn in 1933, Ruth Bader Ginsburg has led a life of
firsts—first in her class at Cornell, first woman on the *Harvard Law
Review*, first tenured female professor at Columbia Law School—and
a very notable second, when in 1993 she became the second woman
named to the Supreme Court. The justice's legacy has been built upon her
relentless work furthering gender equality and civil rights. In 1971, she
wrote the brief for *Reed v. Reed*, which caused the Supreme Court to ex-
tend the Equal Protection Clause to women. Her dissenting opinion in the
Ledbetter v. Goodyear case inspired President Barack Obama to enact the
Lilly Ledbetter Fair Pay Act in 2009—not to mention brought her
national attention as people rallied behind the message like a battle cry,
culminating in the Notorious RBG "I dissent" meme. Ginsburg also
cofounded the Women's Rights Project at the ACLU and argued multiple
cases before the Supreme Court, proving that gender inequality is harmful to both women and men. And to top it all off, she was the first justice of
the Supreme Court to officiate a same-sex marriage. Long may she reign!

*According to folklore, the first gin cocktail was the Martinez, a close relative
to the Martini. One day in the late 1800s in a chilly San Francisco bar,
bartender Jerry Thomas asked a traveling patron where he was going. When
he replied that he was crossing the bay to Martinez and needed to warm up,
Thomas made him a stiff gin and vermouth cocktail. "Very well," he ex-
claimed, "here is a new cocktail I invented for your trip. We will call it 'the
Martinez.'" That's just a Mar-teeny bit less important than Ginsburg's contributions to history, but hopefully your friends will cit-trust that the story's true and know that you're not just twist-ing their arm.*

VODKA

DiRTY
Bettie-ni PAGE

IN A CHILLED MARTINI GLASS

3 oz VodKA

½ oz dRY VeRMOUTH

½ oz OLive Juice

WANT it XXX-TRA DiRTY? Add
ANOTHER SPLASH of bRINE

to gARNISH,
Stick A "piN-UP"
iNSIDE 3 OLives
& SLide iN tHE gLASS

IF You LUST FOR
ANOTHER FLAVOR, TRY A
+ ✧ gibSON + ✧

A MARTINI WITH A PEARL
ONION bARNISH
gib-SOME LOVE to YouR
taSTE buds

∘Stir | Serve Up∘

BETTIE PAGE

DIRTY BETTIE-NI PAGE (DIRTY MARTINI)

I think you can do your own thing as long as you're not hurting anybody else—that's been my philosophy ever since I was a little girl.

—Bettie Page

Notorious 1950s pinup model Bettie Page is an early American icon of body-positive, sex-positive feminism who has never for an instant gone out of style. After appearing as *Playboy's* Playmate of the Month in 1955, Page continued her modeling career, specializing in nude modeling as well as some female-dominance bondage scenes. Her work was considered pornography, available only through illegal, under-the-counter purchases.

Bettie Page is a feminist icon because she managed to enjoy power and pleasure for her sake. She subjugated the male gaze and felt comfortable in her own skin when few women at that time were able. Plus, she popularized the iconic hairstyle still emulated today, appropriately referred to as "Bettie Bangs"—a jet-black fringe that curves downward into a sexy V in the center of the forehead. (We have a lot to thank her for.) Images of Page are part of the cultural landscape, inspiring a timeless iconic look of sex appeal, empowerment, and even dominance. She challenged the wholesome, cookie-cutter role of a woman as submissive sex object and dared to bend over and spank the status quo.

You can Bettie your bottom dollar she took her Martinis dirty! Try one on for size. Maybe this drink will fit you like a leather glove, with matching push-up bra and garter belt. Here's a brine idea: Why don't you (Bettie) bangs one of these cocktails out and show everyone how it's done? Olive this sex talk has gotten me thirsty.

Mosc-NOW Mule

IN A HiGHbALL WiTH iCE

2 oz VodKA
1/2 oz Lime Juice
top WiTH ginger beer*

gARNiSH WiTH Lime Wedge
& cANdied ginger

Serve on a cocktail napkin

555- NOW

*iF YOU don't WANT
store-bought ginger beer,
gather a crew and make
YOUR OWN ginger simple
SYRUP

• 1 PART: fresh ginger juice
• 1 PART: SugAR
• 2 PARTS: Hot WATER

Add 1 oz SYRUP to dRiNK
& top WiTH SOdA WATER

NATIONAL ORGANIZATION FOR WOMEN (NOW)

MOSC-NOW MULE (MOSCOW MULE)

With thousands of members and more than five hundred chapters, the National Organization for Women (NOW) helped write the book on grassroots organizing in the United States. The group was formed in 1966 by a small group of women (among them Betty Friedan, Shirley Chisholm, and Muriel Fox) who attended the National Conference of Commissions on the Status of Women. During the conference, multiple delegates were denied an opportunity to make a legal case for ending workplace discrimination based on gender. Instead of giving up, fifteen to twenty women met that evening to discuss alternative plans of action. Famous in the history of this organization was when Friedan scribbled "NOW" on a napkin and covertly passed it to the other women. They soon made the leap to actual paper and drafted a "Statement of Purpose" that confronted the need for equal opportunity among sexes and genders.

Although it's slightly dated, many discriminatory practices defined by this manifesto are still relevant, sadly. And yet, NOW's work has brought plenty of victories, from enforcing laws for equal job opportunities; to fighting for greater funding and access to child care, reproductive health, and maternity leave benefits; to working toward ending violence against women. The sustained membership and achievements of NOW prove that grassroots organizing and voluntary civic engagement can bring about meaningful change.

Mules are wonderful creatures that know how to carry a heavy load and demand what's best for them. Some may say they're stubborn, but they're really just strong-willed and unafraid to resist if things don't sit right with them. Try channeling the mule when you make this drink. Or when you form a multinational organization dedicated to a revolution of human rights. Okay, go get drunk. NOW. When you finally try it, mule see what all the fuss is about.

Sweet Flanner-tea O'Connor

IN A PITCHER
(STANDARD 48oz)

- 8oz Vodka
- 1½ oz triple Sec
- 1 oz Lemon Juice
- ~26oz BLACK teA* (CHILLED)

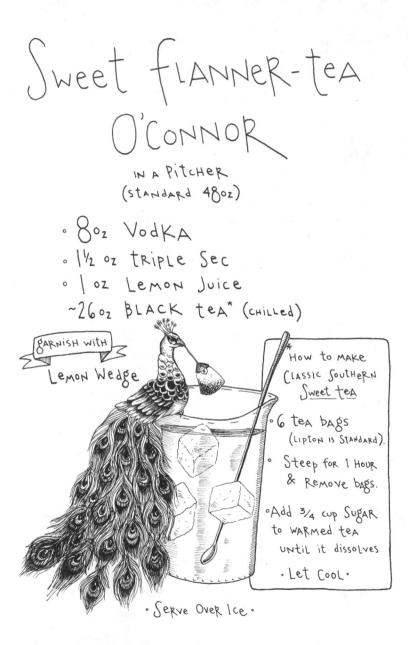

GARNISH WITH

Lemon Wedge

* How to Make Classic Southern Sweet teA

- 6 tea bags (Lipton is Standard).
- Steep for 1 Hour & Remove bags.
- Add ¾ cup Sugar to warmed teA until it dissolves
- · Let Cool ·

· Serve Over Ice ·

FLANNERY O'CONNOR

SWEET FLANNER-TEA O'CONNOR (JOHN DALY)

*I don't deserve any credit for turning the other cheek as my
tongue is always in it.* —Flannery O'Connor

With a penchant for dark humor and sly irony, Flannery O'Connor is considered one of the finest American authors in the Southern Gothic tradition. She was born in Savannah, Georgia, in 1925 and raised in a Catholic household, and both her upbringing and her faith profoundly influenced her work.

O'Connor graduated from the famed Iowa Writers' Workshop in 1947, going on to publish two novels and more than thirty short stories in her short lifetime. She won the Rinehart-Iowa Fiction Award in 1947 and was posthumously awarded the National Book Award for Fiction in 1972. Her works examine the faith journey of her characters, and her writing's apocalyptic underpinnings were presented as completely commonplace, like tying one's shoes or sipping one's boozy iced tea. Her profoundly moving work gave a rare glimpse into the intersection of beauty, irony, and the dark underbelly of humanity. Throughout many of her stories, O'Connor references the peacock, and she even spent the last years of her life surrounded by the majestic birds. Her fondness for the bird and its repeated symbolic occurrences in her stories offer a reminder that grace and beauty are at work in the world, even amid ugliness. O'Connor died tragically at the age of thirty-nine after a long battle with lupus, but even with a life cut so short, she left behind an impressive body of work and a unique, untouchable perspective on the human experience.

They say O'Connor liked to drink Coca-Cola mixed with coffee, but if that combo doesn't tickle you, try adding just a splash of Coke into your cocktail. Mixed with black tea, it'll give you the caffeine jolt and cut the bitterness. Or try her version if you want—imitation is the sincerest form of Flannery.

BLOODY MARY
WOLL-STOUT-CRAFT

IN A PINT GLASS
WITH ICE

- 2 oz VODKA
- 6 oz TOMATO JUICE

STIR IN...

- 1/2 oz LEMON JUICE
- 1/2 oz WORCESTERSHIRE SAUCE
- 1/4 oz HORSERADISH (PREPARED)
- 1/4 oz PICKLE JUICE
- 4-6 DASHES OF TABASCO

PINCH OF...

BLACK PEPPER,
OLD BAY, CAYENNE **...to taste**

- top with STOUT BEER FLOAT

GARNISH WITH OLIVE, CORNICHON,
CELERY, LEMON & MANIFESTO
SIGNED IN BLOOD (OPTIONAL)

MARY WOLLSTONECRAFT

BLOODY MARY WOLL-STOUT-CRAFT (BLOODY MARY)

Taught from infancy that beauty is woman's scepter, the mind shapes itself to the body, and roaming round its gilt cage, only seeks to adorn its prison. —Mary Wollstonecraft

In general, the late 1700s was not the most receptive era for groundbreaking feminist theory. As the author of *A Vindication of the Rights of Woman*, as well as many other treatises, novels, and books of conduct, Mary Wollstonecraft threw down challenges that flew in the face of her society's norms.

Wollstonecraft fought for rights that would allow women to be active and equal partners in society and relationships and urged them to own their sexuality. In her unfinished novel *Maria, or The Wrongs of Woman*, Wollstonecraft put forth the daring argument that women had strong sexual desires, too, and that to ignore them was immoral and degrading (and probably a missed opportunity for men in the Georgian era, although Wollstonecraft didn't necessarily say so).

Wollstonecraft was a writer and philosopher who demanded education for women—not to make them more attractive for men but because real education could lead to a society where men and women were seen as equals. As you might expect, this unpopular mission earned her a nasty reputation. Mary Wollstonecraft's revolutionary thoughts were met with nothing but controversy, but in her works were the seeds of the movements to come. Centuries later, she has become a cornerstone of early feminist philosophy.

This is a bold drink—daring, tough, and spicy as hell. Introducing a splash of stout beer rounds it out, creating a cocktail that is logical, balanced, and thoughtful, much like Ms. Wollstonecraft. Eat, drink, and be Mary, for tomorrow we may die!

Long Island iced LGB-tea-q

IN A PINT GLASS

3/4 oz Vodka
3/4 oz Gin
3/4 oz White Rum
3/4 oz Tequila
3/4 oz Triple Sec
1/2 oz Lemon Juice

GARNISH WITH
A LEMON WEDGE & RAINBOW SKITTLES

·SHAKE· TOP WITH COLA·

LGBTQ RIGHTS MOVEMENT

LONG ISLAND ICED LGB-TEA-Q (LONG ISLAND ICED TEA)

No person is your friend who demands your silence, or denies your right to grow. —Alice Walker

Since the 1950s (and long before, though with less widespread coverage) the American lesbian, gay, bisexual, transgender, and queer (LGBTQ) community has been fighting for inclusion, acceptance, and the rights afforded all people. After decades of small and large victories, the movement continues to gain more allies and greater visibility.

Beginning with the Mattachine Society and the Daughters of Bilitis, LGBTQ people have publicly organized for the protection of queer communities. Such groups rose to prominence at a time when being gay was a crime punishable by law, and the importance of challenging discrimination and building a community has always been at the heart of their action. The Stonewall Riots in 1969 galvanized these communities to make the nation aware of their existence, and let the world know they were not going away.

There are still battles to be fought for visibility, acceptance, and equal rights on all fronts. The LGBTQ community and their allies continue to rally against so-called bathroom bills, discrimination in employment, and damaging social stigma. But every day, LGBTQ crusaders, activists, volunteers, and allies make headway in their fight, and slowly, we are moving toward a more accepting society. Acknowledgment, tolerance, and acceptance—let's drink to that!

Served on the rocks, or Stone Walls, this drink combines every clear, queer spirit in your well. Mix it all up, splash it with a little sweet, a little sour, and you've got yourself everything under the rainbow in one tall glass. Time to come out and GIVE 'EM HELL-GBTQ!

Weather

Under-Greyhound

In a Highball

- 2 oz Vodka
- 2 oz Grapefruit juice
- 1/4 oz Lemon Juice
- 1/4 oz Simple Syrup
- 1 pinch of Kosher Salt

- Shake · Serve over Ice ·
top with Soda Water

Garnish with Lime Wedge

For Gray clouds without the stormy weather, salt & pepper the Rim of Your Glass

BERNARDINE DOHRN

The aspects of patriotism that hush dissent, encourage going along, and sanction comfortable distancing and compliance with what is indecent and unacceptable . . . are too fundamental to ignore or gloss over.
—Bernardine Dohrn

Bernardine Dohrn was a prominent student organizer who helped found the Weather Underground, a left-wing, radical, and black power organization. The group known as the Weathermen was formed by the Students for a Democratic Society (SDS) in opposition to the Vietnam War. The group took a direct-action, militant, and socialist approach to challenge what they perceived as a corrupt government built on classist, capitalist organization. Dohrn's work landed her on the FBI's Ten Most Wanted Fugitives list, forcing her to live on the run for a decade.

Dohrn and her husband emerged from hiding in 1980 and turned themselves in to the FBI, only to find that most charges against them had been dropped due to illegal wiretapping. After serving three years' probation, Dohrn joined a prestigious Chicago law practice, where she befriended, among other prominent activists, Michelle Obama, a fellow attorney at the firm. In addition to her work in law, Dohrn is a board member of numerous human rights organizations, including heading the Children and Family Justice Center at Northwestern University, where she champions the needs of adolescents and their families using a leftist, socialist academic framework. Her many years living and working underground may have put her off the map, but they also planted seeds and helped grow a movement.

Like the racing dog it's named after, this cocktail is diligent, quick, savvy, and packs a punch. It's tart, acidic, and not always gentle, but it's a gosh Dohrn charmer! Weather you're Underground or aboveground, this cocktail will never be revolt-ing.

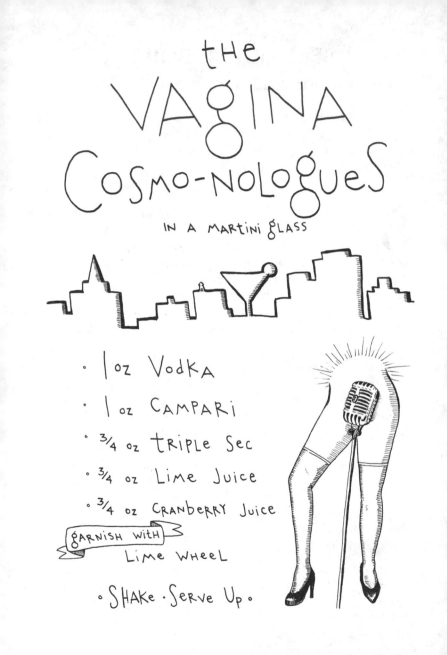

the VAGINA Cosmo-NologueS

IN A MARTINI GLASS

- 1 oz VodkA
- 1 oz CAMPARI
- 3/4 oz tRiPLe SeC
- 3/4 oz LiMe JuICe
- 3/4 oz CRANBeRRY JuICe

GARNiSH WitH LiMe WHeeL

• SHAKe • SeRve UP •

THE VAGINA MONOLOGUES

VAGINA COSMO-NOLOGUES (CAMPARI COSMOPOLITAN)

> *I bet you're worried. I was worried. I was worried about vaginas. I was worried about what we think about vaginas, and even more worried that we don't think about them.*
>
> —Eve Ensler, *The Vagina Monologues*

Eve Ensler's *The Vagina Monologues* debuted in New York City in 1996. Originally an episodic monologue performed by the author, it has since transformed into an ensemble show. Ensler interviewed two hundred women about their vaginas, shaping their stories into dramatic pieces that deal with the feminine experience. In monologues like "My Angry Vagina," "My Vagina Was My Village," "Reclaiming Cunt," and "The Woman Who Loved to Make Vaginas Happy," characters share a whole range of experiences. The play touches on difficult subjects like rape and genital mutilation, and the once-taboo topics of menstruation and masturbation, while also celebrating love and, of course, the joy of orgasm. Ensler's initial intention—to celebrate the vagina and femininity—evolved into a movement to stop violence against women through annual V-Day events.

There's still a long road ahead before the beautiful variety of female (and transgender-inclusive) anatomy isn't seen as a taboo, a dirty word, or merely a sex object, but *The Vagina Monologues*'s willingness to celebrate rather than censor the vag, in all of its natural wonder, certainly helps set the stage.

Stage fright? Have a couple of these drinks and you'll be up there, fist raised high, exclaiming "Vulva la Revolution!" in no time. I'd give you a Cosmopoliten out of ten.

Alexandra Kahlúa'ntai

IN AN OLD FASHIONED GLASS
WITH ICE

1 ½ oz RUSSIAN VODKA

1 oz KAHLÚA

top WITH HALF & HALF

FIERCELY SKEWER A RED CHERRY

ALEXANDRA KOLLONTAI

ALEXANDRA KAHLÚA'NTAI (WHITE RUSSIAN)

It is . . . only in union with the working women and men of the whole world, that we will achieve a new and brighter future— the socialist brotherhood of the workers.

—Alexandra Kollontai

Alexandra Kollontai was a Bolshevik revolutionary, a Marxist, and an early feminist. She became politically active in the 1890s as a member of the St. Petersburg Mobile Museum of Teaching Aids, an underground group that offered classes to factory workers and raised funds to support people during labor strikes.

Through her work, Kollontai recognized the separation that existed between the bourgeois women of the establishment and the working women of the proletariat, and she looked for ways to unite them under the common cause of feminism. The result of this effort was *The Social Basis of the Woman Question*, a Marxist primer on the oppression of women with lessons on how to organize and resist.

After the Russian Revolution of 1917, Kollontai was appointed commissar for social welfare and became the only female member of the Bolshevik government. During these years, she began writing about the theory of sexual politics, fighting for free love and challenging the idea of the nuclear family, as it perpetuated classist and sexist ideals. Kollontai's ideas on sexual liberation and politics reemerged in the 1960s and '70s, when her work was celebrated by many prominent voices in the United States who echoed her call for liberation.

This drink quenches thirst and provides strength. Okay, not really, but the calcium in milk keeps a body strong and alert, and the vodka sends a jolt of Russian Bolshevik Revolution surging through your veins. Plus, Kahlúa makes you feel sexy. Stay the night and I'll Kahlúa taxi in the morning.

Anne Sexton the Beach

IN A HIGHBALL

2 oz BLUEBERRY VODKA
(REGULAR VODKA WORKS FINE — JUST ADD A DASH MORE FRUIT LIQUEUR, OR KEEP AS IS)

1/2 oz CRÈME de CASSIS

1/2 oz DRY VERMOUTH

1 oz CRANBERRY JUICE

1 oz ORANGE JUICE

GARNISH WITH A BLUEBERRY & UMBRELLA

SHAKE.
STRAIN OVER ICE.

ANNE SEXTON

ANNE SEXTON THE BEACH (SEX ON THE BEACH)

A woman who writes feels too much.

—Anne Sexton

Anne Sexton's work dared to address topics considered taboo for poetry, including menstruation, abortion, masturbation, adultery, incest, and drug addiction. Her fearlessness both enticed and repelled readers when she published *To Bedlam and Part Way Back* in 1960. In it, she spoke of her struggles with mental illness and attempts at recovery. Her work was raw, painful, honest, and beautiful.

Sexton's writing career began when her therapist encouraged her to write about what she was feeling, thinking, and dreaming between sessions. She soon found a home among the Boston writing scene, working with contemporaries Sylvia Plath, George Starbuck, Robert Lowell, and Beatrice Berg. Among her many honors and awards is a Pulitzer Prize for Poetry, awarded in 1967 for her book *Live or Die*.

After years of battling depression and multiple institutionalizations, Sexton took her own life on October 4, 1974. Her work continues to inspire poets and readers, who find solace in her ability to articulate the darkest struggles of human existence, where, for most of us, words fail.

Even in stormy weather, waves violently crashing, dark clouds all-encompassing, there is an inexplicable comfort brought on by the vastness of the sea. Poetic as it may be, it is also a great place to forget your troubles with a stiff drink. Raise your glass to an artist who truly helped bring out the beauty in darkness; because, let's face it, life can be a real beach.

DIAN FOSSEY
NAVEL

IN A HIGHBALL

- 1 ½ oz VODKA
- ½ oz PEACH SCHNAPPS
- 1 oz ORANGE JUICE
- 2 DASHES PEYCHAUD'S BITTERS
- BAR SPOON OF POMEGRANATE MOLASSES*

*HEAT POMEGRANATE JUICE IN SAUCEPAN WITH SMALL SPLASH OF BALSAMIC VINEGAR & PINCH OF SUGAR UNTIL IT REDUCES TO SYRUP.

GARNISH WITH AN ORANGE OR PEACH SLICE — AS A PEACH OFFERING

· SHAKE ·

STRAIN OVER ICE

DIAN FOSSEY

DIAN FOSSEY NAVEL (FUZZY NAVEL/MONKEY GLAND)

When you realize the value of all life, you dwell less on what is past and concentrate more on the preservation of the future.
—Dian Fossey

One of the most respected primatologists of all time, Dian Fossey galvanized support for the plight of the mountain gorillas of Rwanda and the Congo. Fossey, like her friend Jane Goodall, attributed the gorillas' acceptance of her to her complete immersion into their habitat. For eighteen years, Fossey lived among the gorillas in harsh conditions, leading the locals to give her the name "Nyiramacibiri," or "The Woman Who Lives Alone on the Mountain."

Fossey was a fierce opponent of poachers and their corrupt arrangements with park rangers, and she eventually set up her own anti-poaching brigades. They disrupted poaching every way they could—including shaming, punishing, and prosecuting offenders. She was also a vocal opponent of ecotourism because of the destruction it wreaked on the delicate ecological systems she studied. Fossey took a more radical approach than others in her field, which heightened awareness of environmental issues and inspired others to employ similar activism tactics. But it also earned her numerous (and well-funded) enemies.

Sadly, Dian Fossey was found murdered in her cabin in 1985, and the crime remains unsolved. To honor her life's work and passions, her foundation continues to monitor, protect, and nurture gorilla populations with many other impactful conservation projects worldwide.

This cocktail's the full package. It will enliven your senses and stimulate your ape-tite. It will give you warm Fosseys and offer you peach of mind. It will put some hair on your chest. And back. And, well, everywhere. It's the gorill-deal.

TEQUILA &
MEZCAL

DOLORES
HUERTA-QUILA
SUNRISE

IN A HIGHBALL WITH ICE

- 2 oz tequila
- top with ORANGE Juice (not quite to the top!)

Float
~ 1 oz Strawberry Shrub

how to make a shrub in advance

2 cups Strawberries
1 cup Sugar
1 cup Water
1 cup Apple cider Vinegar

IN A SAUCEPAN, dissolve sugar in water, then add berries until syrup begins to blend. Let cool & muddle fruit & simple syrup. Store in jar for 1-2 days, add vinegar, stir & strain.

DOLORES HUERTA

DOLORES HUERTA-QUILA SUNRISE
(TEQUILA SUNRISE/SHRUB)

Every moment is an organizing opportunity, every person a
potential activist, every minute a chance to change the world.
—Dolores Huerta

D olores Huerta is one of the most fierce crusaders for human rights in American history. As a spokesperson for voiceless and disenfranchised migrant workers and immigrants, as well as for women and children of Hispanic descent, Huerta has helped us to envision a society where one day workers' rights are honored on all levels and where borders don't define and divide communities.

As the daughter of a coal miner, Huerta grew up with a front-row seat to the challenges that working families in migrant communities faced. Unwilling to ignore the gross economic and gender inequities that existed, Huerta began organizing within her community. In the 1960s, she joined forces with Cesar Chavez to cofound the National Farm Workers Association (NFWA). Her involvement with the NFWA was instrumental in providing greater access to health care and welfare services for migrant workers, all while bringing attention to a population who had been treated as invisible.

In her time as an activist, Huerta led strikes and organized unions; she marched in the streets and was beaten at demonstrations. She has led a life of courage while maintaining a nurturing spirit—not only to her eleven children but also to the entire population of immigrants and migrant workers whom she fights to protect.

The colorful layering of this cocktail is so picturesque, it's like watching the
sun rise before your berry eyes. Even in the darkest hour, if you mix yourself
one of these drinks—it'll soon dawn on you. You're not alone. So make some
more and then pass them around. Huer-together in this fight for equality!

MARGARITA Atwood

IN AN OLD FASHIONED OR MARGARITA GLASS

2 oz TEQUILA

¾ oz COINTREAU

1 oz LIME JUICE

LIME WHEEL

GARNISH WITH

Add a dash of PEYCHAUD'S bitters to the eye of the lime & float it over your drink— it's ALWAYS WATCHING YOU

∘SHAKE∘

Serve over Ice

UNDER HIS EYE AM DRUNK

MARGARET ATWOOD

MARGARITA ATWOOD (MARGARITA)

The answers you get from literature depend on the questions you pose.

—Margaret Atwood

Canadian poet, author, and teacher Margaret Atwood serves up dystopian stories rife with environmental horror, misogyny, and general oppression by an elite ruling class. Her best-known work, *The Handmaid's Tale*, describes an oppressive society that values women only for their ovaries while denying them access to education and equal opportunities. The handmaids in the story must wear bonnets with long cloth wings extending past their cheeks and draping down their faces. Metaphorically, the bonnet reminds us we don't need to hide and cautions us never to avert our eyes.

Whether prophetic or simply observant of history's tendency to repeat itself, Atwood's gift for storytelling gets under the reader's skin and reminds us to be mindful of the way small actions can have grave consequences. She denies that most of her books, including *The Handmaid's Tale*, are actually science fiction and instead says that they are "speculative fiction," because, unlike science fiction, which "has monsters and spaceships," speculative fiction could really happen. Her work underlines the importance of using our platforms—creative or otherwise—to both send a message and stay true to our ethics and morality.

Handmaid in classic Margarita fashion, this cocktail should be shaken up 'til everyone around you takes notice and starts moving in your direction. I don't mean to speculate, but I have a feeling that if you really Marga-read between the limes, you'll understand how, when maiden proper fashion, this drink gained such a high reputation.

eLiXiR- BeTH WARREN

IN A PINT GLASS

MUDDLE 2 WATERMELON SEGMENTS

- 2 oz tequila
- 3/4 oz Lime Juice
- 1/4 oz green chartreuse
- 2 basil Leaves

○ SHAKE ○ "dirty pour" ALL contents
back INTO PINT ○ Add more Ice ○

top WITH tonic WATER
garnish WITH WATERMELON wedge
& basil (SLAP it AROUND —
   to RELEASE oils & put IN its place)

ELIZABETH WARREN

ELIXIR-BETH WARREN (TEQUILA AND TONIC/SMASH)

She was warned. She was given an explanation. Nevertheless,
she persisted. —Mitch McConnell

I n 2017, Massachusetts senator Elizabeth Warren was opposing the nomination of Jeff Sessions for attorney general when Senate Majority Leader Mitch McConnell publicly silenced her. During her speech, Warren cited a 1986 opposition letter written by Coretta Scott King, criticizing Sessions's failure to defend anti-segregation voting laws. McConnell's response—essentially telling Warren to sit down, shut up, resume proper feminine conduct, or *else*—ignited a firestorm. Warren's calmness in the face of his actions made her a feminist hero to many Americans, and an important force in people-powered politics.

Warren has built her political career fighting for the rights of working- and middle-class people. Her work in the Senate has focused on holding Wall Street and big banking corporations accountable, making her an unofficial "Sheriff of Wall Street." Warren's fearless outspokenness has distinguished her as a leading voice against fraud and corruption at large. Through her actions, she has helped remind us of the importance of staying engaged, staying critical, and staying fired up. We the people have the power to stand up for what we believe in, and we, too, can stand up to the Wall Street bull. . . .

The quinine in tonic has a long history of medicinal effects, so couple it with a serving of fresh basil and tequila, and you'll have the strength to stand up to bullies—be it multinational corporate banking conglomerates, billionaire politicians, or a gnarly hangover. You're basil-y invincible. This drink is so delicious you'll want to elix-your lips and have one or a mellion more. Someone tries to cut you off? Nevertheless, you'll per-sip.

Mez-CoCo CHANeL

NUMERO °5

SERVES TRES - CINCO PERSONAS

2½ cups ORANGE JUICE (20 oz)

1½ cups TOMATO JUICE (12 oz)

4 oz LIME JUICE

½ oz SOY SAUCE

1 oz POMEGRANATE JUICE

2½ oz HOT SAUCE (VALENTINA) OR TAPATIO

ANCHO CHILI POWDER to taste

IN 1ST ROCKS GLASS

1½ oz MEZCAL

IN 2ND ROCKS GLASS

1½ oz SANGRITA

take the SHOT
then
CHASE it!

N°5 CHANEL
AGAVE

PARFUM

COCO CHANEL

MEZ-COCO CHANEL NUMERO 5 (SANGRITA)

Don't spend time beating on a wall, hoping to transform it into a door.

—Coco Chanel

Born in 1883, and raised in an orphanage, Coco Chanel rose to the very height of fashion through talent, intellect, and drive. She arrived on the scene with the eponymous Chanel No. 5 perfume, which is still among the world's most popular fragrances. Her unique design sense led her to perfect the little black dress and her trademark suits, which borrowed elements from men's wear while achieving an entirely feminine line. These revolutionary designs chucked the corsets and confinement of the past in favor of styles that epitomized comfort and grace. She experimented with androgyny and challenged existing ideas of femininity and sex appeal, not just in high fashion but also in mainstream culture.

A romance with a German officer during World War II complicates Chanel's legacy, leaving a nasty stain. And when one's legacy is very literally one of perfect garments, a stain is not a good look. Chanel shut down her house at the outbreak of World War II but reopened it to critical acclaim and financial success in 1954.

Mezcal's robust, smoky flavors can often overpower a cocktail—possibly even offend—but the other steps and ingredients round out this drink nicely. Chanel all your energy into making this concoction perfect and you may become an icon. If it's received in poor taste, don't Mez-call it a day. If it Co-co'mes down to that, just drink alone. In your little black dress. Or your chic suit.

Life of the PATTI

in 3 shot glasses

- 1½ oz tequila blanco - clean, lighter, greener, more youthful flavor

- 1½ oz tequila Reposado - smoother, subtler, more mature, "Rested" older sister

- 1½ oz tequila Añejo - deeper, darker, more complex, aged for more than one year in oak

Although often paired with salt & lime, a quality 100% agave tequila doesn't need training wheels. Here's to pour decisions!

tequila
is the outcast, the Rebel, the black sheep of the spirits. It simultaneously Repels & pleases the palate while the agave base provides a stimulant effect. It's no surprise many associate it with a Rough Night. Once You discover the seductive powers of this subtle beast, You'll be head over heels. Because the Night belongs to Lovers.

PATTI SMITH

LIFE OF THE PATTI (TEQUILA FLIGHT/SHOTS)

Never let go of that fiery sadness called desire.

—Patti Smith

Poet, photographer and visual artist, and punk pioneer Patti Smith has built a career that's taken her to some strange places. Despite having spent the majority of her life surrounded by some of the most influential and undeniably "cool" artists of all time, she never compromised her own unique style, vision, and approach to life to conform to anyone else's.

After a brief stint in college, she skipped out to New York City, pursuing art as a performance poet. She gained a following in the New York art scene, and in 1974, she formed a band to record the seminal punk song "Piss Factory." The Patti Smith Group was fueled by Smith's manic stage presence and powerful lyrics. A string of successful albums followed, but in 1979, Smith married MC5 guitarist Fred "Sonic" Smith and disappeared from public life for many years. Following her husband's death in 1994, Smith returned to the music world and produced another set of celebrated albums.

In 2010, she released the memoir *Just Kids*, which, in addition to recounting her early years in 1960s New York City, was an intimate ode to Robert Mapplethorpe, whom she called "the artist in my life." It went on to win the National Book Award, giving another nod to the legendary bohemian, staunch individual, and American icon.

You're convinced it's out tequila-ya, but it's not. Tequila is your friend. Your punk, nonconformist friend, but your friend through and through. Maybe you were Just Kids the first time you tried it—don't write it off forever. Savor the quality, flavor, subtlety, then allow yourself to get fully pulled into its madness. Then pour another round, shoot 'em back, and become the life of the Patti.

COMANDANTA PALOMA

IN A HIGHBALL WITH ICE

- 2 oz JALAPEÑO-INFUSED* TEQUILA REPOSADO
- 1/2 oz LIME JUICE
- TOP WITH GRAPEFRUIT SODA (TRADITIONALLY MEXICAN SQUIRT BUT ANY WILL DO)

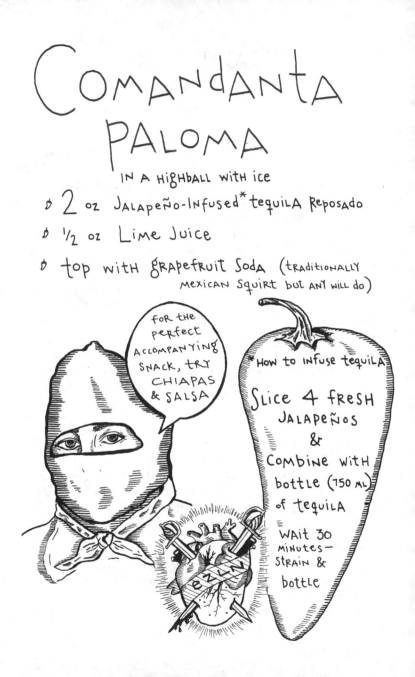

FOR THE PERFECT ACCOMPANYING SNACK, TRY CHIAPAS & SALSA

*HOW TO INFUSE TEQUILA

SLICE 4 FRESH JALAPEÑOS & COMBINE WITH BOTTLE (750 ML) OF TEQUILA

WAIT 30 MINUTES— STRAIN & BOTTLE

COMANDANTA RAMONA

COMANDANTA PALOMA (PALOMA)

Our hope is that one day our situation will change, that we women will be treated with respect, justice, and democracy.
—Comandanta Ramona

Comandanta Ramona was a daring leader of the Ejército Zapatista de Liberación Nacional (EZLN), who planned the 1994 uprising in Chiapas, Mexico. "The Petite Warrior" fought for the rights of indigenous women, who continue to struggle against exploitation and marginalization by the Mexican government. Ramona was the architect of the ten-part "Women's Revolutionary Laws," which made demands for the rights, health, and welfare of women, all while unequivocally stating that women are equal to men. Because of her efforts, the law was adopted by the EZLN as a foundational element of the movement.

Until the end of her life, Comandanta Ramona fought for her people, demanding that the Mexican government comply with the San Andrés Accords agreed upon in 1996. The Accords called for basic respect for the diversity of the indigenous peoples of Chiapas and autonomy over their territories. Despite initially agreeing to the terms, Mexican president Ernesto Zedillo and his military almost immediately reneged. The EZLN, with Comandanta Ramona firmly on the front lines, declared war after their calls for peace were denied. Aligning itself with a larger anti-neoliberal, globalization social movement, the EZLN has taken direct militant action to protect the indigenous people of Chiapas by any means necessary.

Maybe you're a Palom' wolf and prefer to drink by yourself, or maybe when you have a few of these you Comandan' the attention of an entire room. Either way, this drink will give you the strength to stand up to bullies and protect what's yours . . . should anyone try and get jalapeñ-your business.

FRiDA KAHL-aDA

IN A MARGARITA GLASS

2½ oz tequila Añejo
1 oz coconut cream (coco López)
2 oz pineapple juice
½ oz lime juice

1 dash of
vanilla
extract

~ 1 cup crushed ice
or 5-6 cubes

Blend on High
in blender

Garnish with Pineapple
slice & lime wheel

FRIDA KAHLO

FRIDA KAHL-ADA (TEQUILA PIÑA COLADA)

Feet, what do I need you for when I have wings to fly?
—Frida Kahlo

Born Magdalena Carmen Frida Kahlo y Calderón, this mid-twentieth-century Mexican artist is better known as Frida Kahlo. She is famed for her flamboyant lifestyle, her native dress and jewelry, her communist politics, and her surrealist paintings, as well as her tumultuous, on-again, off-again open marriage to muralist and Mexican Communist Party member Diego Rivera. We love her for her groundbreaking paintings and for having the best eyebrows in the history of art.

Kahlo's work was largely informed by a lifelong struggle with physical pain, resulting from childhood polio and a devastating bus accident during her university years. Over the course of her life, Kahlo underwent more than thirty operations. Her transcendent paintings were often self-portraits, which she used to comment on personal and global themes, including sexuality, politics, history, gender, race, class, post-colonialism, pain, illness, and love. In depictions of herself, Kahlo challenged traditional beauty standards by emphasizing the unconventional aspects of her appearance: her prominent brow; her handicapped body; her androgynous, almost masculine features. Kahlo's ability to depict agonizing beauty and peculiar subject matter distinguishes her singular, imaginative style.

Try to imagine what you look like when you drink this cocktail and, from deep in that creative brain of yours, paint a portrait of yourself. You're Frida do what you want with it—it's your self-portrait! And remember, the more of these you drink, the better it will look. Creativity is Kahl-ing to you.

RUM

MiLLION
WO-MiNT
march -ito

IN A HiGHBALL

2 oz RUM (DARK, LiGHT, YOUNG, OLD — ANY KiND YOU LiKE!)

¾ oz LiME JUiCE

1 oz SiMPLE SYRUP &

8 MiNT LEAVES, MUDDLED

SHAKE iT ALL UP!
double STRAiN over ice

NASTY WOMAN!

MiNT GARNiSH!

the future is female

MILLION WOMAN MARCH (WOMEN'S MARCH ON WASHINGTON)

MILLION WO-MINT MARCH-ITO (MOJITO)

The 2017 Women's March on Washington has been called the single largest day of protest in U.S. political history and among the biggest human rights demonstrations worldwide. The protest largely sprang from outrage following the election of a president who had exhibited a dishearteningly misogynistic rhetoric.

While the march was a protest against what felt like a threat to human rights and civil liberties, it was also an appreciation and celebration of WOMAN. People wielded signs of all types: of empowerment, outrage, hope, passion, satire. One of the biggest symbols of the march was the "pussy hat": a knitted pink hat meant to reappropriate the word "pussy" while displaying a visual statement of solidarity.

The march heightened political awareness and encouraged a spirit of organization and unity that persisted long after the sun went down and the barricades were dismantled. The march reintroduced protesting as both a means to vent frustration as well as a way to bring attention to local authorities and news media to issues like women's reproductive rights or outrage caused by police killings of black men and women by groups like Black Lives Matter. More than a celebration, more than a gathering of feminists of all shapes, sizes, genders, religions, and cocktail preferences, it's not just a march—it's a movement.

This drink is mint to be served at a big party. A HUGE party. Like, the biggest one in history. You'll feel it from your head down to your Moji-toes. Hold on to your pussy hat and rum—don't walk! The old world's behind you!

the feminine MYS-tiki

IN A tiki mug

1½ oz DARK RUM

1½ oz WHITE RUM

1 oz 151-PROOF RUM

½ oz FALERNUM

1 tsp GRENADINE &

dash of ANGOSTURA bitters

½ oz CINNAMON Simple SYRUP*

½ oz GRAPEFRUIT juice

¾ oz LIME juice

*for CINNAMON SYRUP PREPARE simple SYRUP AS NORMAL — just ADD 3 cinnamon sticks to boiling WATER before Adding the SUGAR

GARNISH WITH PINEAPPLE, CHERRY, LIME, MINT LEAF & tiki UMBRELLA

• SHAKE •
Serve over crushed ice

BETTY FRIEDAN

THE FEMININE MYS-TIKI (TIKI DRINK/ZOMBIE HOUSEWIFE)

When she stopped conforming to the conventional picture of femininity she finally began to enjoy being a woman.

—Betty Friedan

Betty Friedan is one of the most important intellectual figures of modern feminist theory. Her most widely acclaimed work, *The Feminine Mystique*, was published in 1963 and is often credited as sparking second-wave feminism. Friedan was able to voice a collective, unspoken dissatisfaction with societal expectations for women's lives at that time. Her book explored what she saw as "the problem that has no name": women who were living the life of a housewife in the 1950s and '60s were by and large unhappy.

Later, our girl kept turning the screws on male-dominated ideas of gender conformity by helping establish political action groups like NOW and the National Association for the Repeal of Abortion Laws. Friedan helped organize the Women's Strike for Equality held on August 26, 1970, the fiftieth anniversary of the women's suffrage amendment. She marched in New York City alongside twenty thousand women, demanding equal opportunities in the workplace and academic institutions, as well as "instant revolution against sexual oppression." Though some contemporary activists criticized her views as not progressive enough, it is undeniable that she had a significant impact during this electrifying period of feminist activity and achievement.

Although tiki drinks can be kitschy, they also represent celebration. A tiki drink is a retreat into a joyous, tropical paradise, not some zombie Stepford Wife humdrum. The only zombie here is this cocktail we're dedicating to Betty—one that dares to take you out of the confines of your daily routine and onto the rum-soaked beaches of a warm, happy place full of possibility.

the
BLUEST HAW-eye-AN

IN A HURRICANE GLASS

- 1 oz white Rum
- 1 oz Vodka
- 3/4 oz blue Curaçao
- 2 oz Pineapple Juice
- 1/2 oz Lime Juice
- 3/4 oz coconut cream (Coco López)

GARNISH WITH

ORANGE Slice,
A CHERRY &
UMBRELLA

- SHAKE · Serve Over Ice ·

TONI MORRISON

THE BLUEST HAW-EYE-AN (BLUE HAWAIIAN)

*I don't subscribe to patriarchy, and I don't think it should be
substituted with matriarchy. I think it's a question of equitable
access, and opening doors to all sorts of things.*

—Toni Morrison

Toni Morrison's writing spans many forms, from poetry to librettos, children's books to plays, but her novels have earned her the greatest acclaim. In these, she creates characters that feel alive with both rough edges and profound beauty. They exist across boundaries, between myth and the fantastic, possessing soulful depth and political awareness. *The Bluest Eye*, one of her most controversial works, follows the life of Pecola, a young black girl ridiculed for her dark skin, whose obsession with having blue eyes ultimately leads to her complete alienation and disillusionment. It is one of the American Library Association's most challenged books and has been banned from countless curricula for its depictions of racism, rape, and incest.

In 1988, Morrison won the Pulitzer Prize for her most well-known book *Beloved*, and her literary legacy was cemented when she was awarded the 1993 Nobel Prize in Literature for her lifelong body of work. Her authentic prose and elegant candor have made her a literary icon; but Toni Morrison's truest legacy is perhaps in how she dared to examine the whole complexity of black life in a larger context in the United States, both as an author and as a woman in the public eye.

Whether you're drinking this cocktail because you're feeling blue, you were craving it out of the blue, you're sick of society's narrow blue-ty standards, you enjoy it alongside a flower in blue-m, or you blue your savings on a trip to Hawaii, this is the drink for blue! Er, you. Have one Toni'ght, and then have some Morrison tomorrow.

grog-uerrilla girls

IN A double old fashioned glass

1	oz	Aged Rum
1	oz	DARK RUM
1	oz	white Rum
3/4	oz	grapefruit juice
3/4	oz	Lime Juice
3/4	oz	HONEY SYRUP

use crushed ice to form A SMALL
fine-ART ice Sculpture
◊ freeze in advance ◊

○ SHAKE ○ POUR over your masterpiece ○
(OR LARGE Rocks)

GUERRILLA GIRLS

GROG-UERRILLA GIRLS (NAVY GROG)

The Guerrilla Girls is an anonymous collective of female activists formed in the 1980s. Their goal is to fight gender discrimination within the art world. Donning gorilla masks and using pseudonyms that honor deceased female artists, this collective aims to promote a fuller understanding of how women have been viewed as a subject of art versus how women as creators have consistently been misrepresented.

Utilizing billboards, large-scale installations, posters, printed ephemera, performance art, and surprise public appearances, the Guerrilla Girls force people to recognize the contributions of female artists who have been hugely underrepresented compared to their male counterparts in the art world. Using elements of the absurd, they become a performative piece of art themselves, harnessing this self-awareness to critique larger issues about representation. Their mission to reduce disparities and promote feminism within the arts remains relevant and heralded more than thirty years after they have launched.

When you're not getting recognized as the artistic genius that you are and the Grog-oing gets tough, pound your chest, dress up in a costume, and throw a couple of these bad girls (silver) back. They'll lift your spirits and are easel-ly the most delicious drink you'll ever try—even if consumed through a gorilla mask (but you may want to use a straw).

JOAN of ARC & STORMY

IN A HIGHBALL with ice

◊ POUR ¾-FULL GLASS OF
   ginger beer

◊ 2 OZ DARK SPICED RUM

   FLOAT THE RUM ON TOP
   to CREATE A LAYERED
   COCKTAIL

◊ top WITH A DROP OF
   AbSINTHE

SKEWER A LIME WEDGE RIGHT THROUGH
THE HEART

JOAN OF ARC

JOAN OF ARC & STORMY (DARK & STORMY)

I am not afraid. I was born to do this.   —Joan of Arc

J oan of Arc was a peasant from Normandy, France, who helped lead an army and united her people—all before the age of nineteen. Centuries later, Joan of Arc is still a beloved symbol of French unity and patriotism.

Born in the fifteenth century during the Hundred Years' War, young Joan started hearing voices and seeing visions at the age of thirteen. She believed God was urging her to fight for her people and restore the Kingdom of France, so she donned some armor to conceal her gender and jumped into battle. After winning a series of battles over the English, Joan attracted a group of devout followers who were impressed that God was speaking to her. They followed her into combat, even after discovering she was a teenage girl.

Joan was eventually taken prisoner by the English, who ruthlessly punished her for defying orders and leading a political revolt. She was condemned to execution for dressing in men's clothing and practicing sorcery, and at nineteen, she was tried and found guilty of heresy and ordered to burn at the stake. Twenty-five years after her death, the pope held a new trial, declaring her an innocent martyr. In 1920, the Catholic Church named her a saint.

Joan of Arc embodies courage, strength, perseverance, and resistance. Or, ya know, *résistance*. Her legacy is that of a leader and an emblem of hope during dark and stormy times.

Legend has it, Joan's heart remained unscathed when she was burned. Heart to believe, but it makes for a good story. Go ahead, raise a drink to her—it doesn't really martyr what drink you raise in her honor, as long as there's enough booze in it to fuel a fire.

WILMA'S MANKILLER

IN A HURRICANE GLASS OR SNIFTER

3/4 oz Aged Rum

3/4 oz Dark Rum

3/4 oz Scotch

2 oz Pineapple Juice

1 oz Orange Juice

1 oz Coconut Cream (Coco López)

GARNISH WITH ground nutmeg, pineapple slice & a cherry

∘ HARD SHAKE   Serve over Ice ∘

WILMA MANKILLER

WILMA'S MANKILLER (PAINKILLER)

Everybody is sitting around saying, "Well, jeez, we need some-
body to solve this problem of bias." That somebody is us. We
all have to try to figure out a better way to get along.

—Wilma Mankiller

Wilma Mankiller was born in 1945 on a Native American res-
ervation in Oklahoma. Though her family had no running
water or electricity, Mankiller maintained that she never felt
impoverished. All of that changed when the U.S. Bureau of Indian Affairs relocated her family to San Francisco. The displacement from her
native lands into destitution at the hands of the U.S. government
opened her eyes to the unjust treatment of native peoples and inspired
her lifelong devotion to community and activism.

After decades of activism and service, Wilma Mankiller was elected the
first female chief of a Native American nation in 1983. Mankiller
worked to improve housing and education and built alliances within
the government. During her tenure, the Cherokee Nation population
more than doubled; the relationship between the Cherokee Nation and
the U.S. government strengthened; she published bestselling books
and taught as a professor at Dartmouth; and President Bill Clinton
awarded her the Presidential Medal of Freedom. It's clear that Wilma
Mankiller was no "man killer"—she was a forger of nonviolent alliances. She saw the potential for a better future and worked relentlessly
over the course of her career to build a better life for her people.

The Chero-key to making Wilma's Mankiller is encouraging alliances be-
tween the different ingredients so one doesn't overpower the rest. The bit of
smokiness from the scotch is an unusual addition to the Painkiller, but it
works! Chiefly, it is a harmonious union and blending of strong flavors.

ARTEMIS PUNCH

IN A SCORPION BOWL
(SERVES 4-6 GODS, GODDESSES & MORTALS)

- 3 OZ   WHITE RUM
- 3 OZ   DARK RUM
- 3 OZ   GIN
- 2 OZ   TRIPLE SEC
- 2 OZ   LEMON JUICE
- 4 OZ   NECTAR OF THE GODS
  (ORANGE JUICE WILL DO THE TRICK)
- 1 OZ   POMEGRANATE JUICE

IF YOUR BOWL HAS A VOLCANO IN THE CENTER, FILL THE CUP WITH 1 OZ 151-PROOF RUM & SET ABLAZE.

- STIR TOGETHER WITH ICE -

ARTEMIS

T'ARTEMIS PUNCH (RUM PUNCH)

As the Goddess of the Hunt, Moon Goddess, protector of women and fertility, and guardian of the natural world, Artemis is a heavy hitter in the world of Greek mythology. She's also referred to as "the Lady of Wild Things" and "Mistress of Beasts," because allegedly she would dress up like a bear covered in furs and dance around town. Girl knew how to party! Besides knowing how to shoot a mean arrow, she also protected (and accepted pleasures from) priestesses and nymphs. Artemis supposedly disliked men and often punished or killed them for looking at her sideways. (Okay, that's a little extreme, but we can't all be perfect.) When she met the great huntsman and most handsome man in the world, Orion, she developed a deep bond and revealed her capacity for earnest friendship and love. When Artemis's jealous brother Apollo learned of their friendship, he sent a scorpion to hunt Orion and tricked his sister into killing her friend. She was devastated by the deception and the loss of her friend; in tribute, she placed Orion in the stars next to a small scorpion, which served as a reminder to all mortals to be wary of false company. Who knows—maybe this inspired the invention of the scorpion bowl as a delightfully festive vessel for carrying alcoholic punch. That part isn't officially written into Greek mythology, but let's just go with it.

This drink, like our Goddess of the Hunt, certainly packs a punch: a nice dose of lime will make you purse your lips as a reminder that life's not always as sweet as ambrosia. Hunt down your nearest and deer-est friends and thank Goddess for rum! You're going to love this drink; it's written in the stars. Orion earth are you still sitting here?! Start making this punch!

WANGARI
MAI TAI
IN A HIGHBALL

1 oz white rum
1 oz dark rum
1 oz lime juice
1/2 oz orange curaçao
1/2 oz orgeat syrup*

garnish with
a mint sprig
(or one million)

SHAKE   Serve over ice

*CAN substitute ALMOND-FLAVORED SYRUP

WANGARI MAATHAI

WANGARI MAI TAI (MAI TAI)

It's the little things citizens do. That's what will make the difference. My little thing is planting trees.

—Wangari Maathai

Wangari Maathai was instrumental in teaching rural Kenyan women to improve their lives through conservation and education. Renowned for her efforts to promote democracy, human rights, and environmental awareness, Maathai founded the Green Belt Movement in 1977 to help heal the environment and combat deforestation by planting trees. In later years, she helped the Movement grow beyond its Kenyan roots by creating the Pan-African Green Belt Movement to spread these lessons and methodologies to people in need across the continent.

Maathai also branched out into political work. As cochair of the Jubilee 2000 Africa Campaign, she lobbied for the cancellation of unpayable debt for African countries. In 2002, she won a seat in parliament with 98 percent of her district's votes. She was later named the assistant minister in the Ministry for Environment and Natural Resources. In 2004, Wangari became the first African woman awarded a Nobel Peace Prize.

If this isn't the absolute best Mai Tai (or at least Wan of the tastiest) you've ever had, I promise I'll leaf you alone. Branch out and tree-t yourself. And while you're at it, plant some seeds and abolish the pa-tree-archy. Sorry, that was acorny joke.

Free the ☀ Hot ☀ Buttery Nipple

IN A SAUCEPAN (serves 4)

BEAT OR BLEND

   2 sticks salted butter, softened

   4 tsp mixed baking spices

   try: cloves, ginger, nutmeg, cinnamon, allspice

   3 tsp brown sugar

IN A MUG

   2 oz dark aged rum
   2 tbsp spiced butter
   top with boiling water

° STIR WITH CINNAMON STICK °

FREE THE NIPPLE

FREE THE HOT BUTTERY NIPPLE
(HOT BUTTERY NIPPLE/BUTTERED RUM)

*You know, they sexualize the female body, but the moment a
woman makes a statement with it, we're seemingly commit-
ting a crime.* —Lina Esco

I n the 2014 film *Free the Nipple*, director and creator Lina Esco confronts the societal norms that try to shame and control women's
bodies. Lina dares to ask "Why?"—why is it okay to depict crime,
violence, blatant sexual innuendo, and even male nipples in public,
unsolicited consumerism, but female nipples are a total taboo?

The Free the Nipple movement tackles the inherent hypocrisies women
face over the exposure of female breasts in public and online. Women
online have taken to protesting against "graphic content" policies (i.e.,
any picture that shows a woman's areola) by Photoshopping men's
nipples over their own.

While three states criminalize the mere sight of a woman's breast
(Utah, Kentucky, and Indiana), local statutes make a confusing legal
mess for anyone practicing "top freedom." This movement, which uses
the ubiquitous #freethenipple hashtag, is a modern-day iteration of
the same critique on sexuality and beauty culture that has existed for
centuries—not to mention an encouraging symbol of the power of
social media as a platform to rally behind a collective cause and dis-
courage censorship at large.

*Since the original Buttery Nipple shot is outdated and, well, pretty gross,
peep this take on hot buttered rum. Once people get wind of this drink, it
will send a nipple effect into the ether. After a few, you'll feel free as a bird.
Or free as a (not-contingent-on-sex) nipple. Butter get used to it. They're
here to stay.*

DAIQUI-gAWeA

IN A CHILLED COUPE

- 2 oz RUM (WHITE OR AGED)

- 1 oz LIME JUICE

- 3/4 oz SIMPLE SYRUP

gARNISH WITH LIME WHEEL & AN HERB
FORAGED FROM YOUR gARDEN

· SHAKE · SERVE UP ·

don't get dAiquiR-ied
AWAY — THIS CLASSIC
COCKTAIL is best HONORED
IN ITS SIMPLICITY. YOU
CAN LEAD A HUMAN TO
RUM, bUT YOU CAN'T
MAKE THEM THINK.

SACAGAWEA

DAIQUI-GAWEA (DAIQUIRI)

S acagawea was a translator, explorer, companion, guide, naturalist, and mother. Born into the Shoshone tribe in the 1780s, she spent her first few years peacefully inhabiting the lands of what is now Idaho. But her happy upbringing was short-lived, as she was kidnapped and spent much of her young adulthood being traded and enslaved. She was eventually traded to a French-Canadian fur trader named Toussaint Charbonneau and became his wife and the mother to his child. Together they joined the Corps of Discovery, led by Meriwether Lewis and William Clark, who were tasked by President Jefferson with finding the rumored Northwest Passage. Sacagawea was invaluable to the Corps with her knowledge of the terrain, navigation, resourcefulness, and survival techniques. During her time with Lewis and Clark, she facilitated successful trades, identified plants, and eased tension with various Native American tribes.

Sacagawea is an integral figure in America's history, and it is important to celebrate her. That said, we should remember the true background of her story: she was in essence a poster child for a centuries-old propaganda story, where the Americans were the heroes and the "good" native people were their friends and allies. The more accurate admission is that many of these early settlers, like those who enslaved Sacagawea, were imperialists who participated in a genocide. That is why we must honor her life and contributions to peacemaking. She was clever, kindhearted, and brave—you gotta Saca-to her.

Sacagawea was no rum-of-the-mill person. Let's raise this most classic and timeless of cocktails to the rights of the indigenous people of past and present— and to tell oppressors to "Daiq off!" Then trade, and share, and forage for more cool ingredients! Let's get Loose and Clark tonight.

BRANDY & COGNAC

Amber Jack Rose

IN A SMALL ROCKS GLASS

- 1 ½ oz AppleJack
- ½ oz Light Rum
- ½ oz Lemon Juice
- ½ oz Rose's Grenadine

GARNISH WITH A
CHERRY
(OR TWO — NO SHAME!)

•SHAKE•
Serve Up

AMBER ROSE

AMBER JACK ROSE (JACK ROSE)

We're painting a picture of what everybody already says about us. They call us sluts and whores all the time, so we just embrace it. I have slut written across my vagina. —Amber Rose

The word "slut" is used to make women feel ashamed of their sexuality, categorize them as objects to be used or consumed by men, turn women against one another, and blame those who have been victims of sexual violence. Amber Rose has been in the public eye as an entertainer, initially gaining attention after appearing in Young Jeezy and Kanye West's music video "Put On," before launching a career in modeling, acting, and rapping. Likewise, Rose is largely famous for putting her sexuality on display. She has been publicly slut-shamed by the media, strangers, and her exes, and in response, she has made a loud and conscious effort to take a stand for sex positivity.

In 2015, Rose rallied behind SlutWalk, a movement that began in 2011 to protest the excusing of rape and sexual assault based on the way women dress or behave. She helped bring SlutWalk to a broader audience by leading the event in L.A. in coordination with her nonprofit organization. She has gone on to brand the event, sell tickets, and secure high-profile sponsors. Although she has received criticism for her use of a cause to benefit her own fame, her enormous influence in encouraging conversation around acceptance and empowerment is not to be discredited. Amber Rose makes it her mission to be unapologetic about her sexuality and is a spokesperson for other women to reject that same double standard and truly own their bodies. Take her lead. Is someone making you feel ashamed for how you dress or act? Tell them to put up or slut up.

There's Amber-ning question that needs to be answered: How good is this drink? There's only one way to find out. If you have too many, don't worry; just Walk it off.

BIRTH COINTREAU'L

IN A COCKTAIL GLASS

- 1½ OZ COGNAC
- 3/4 OZ COINTREAU
- 3/4 OZ LEMON JUICE

GARNISH WITH

- ORANGE twist

&

- dARK CHOCOLATE
(OR PREFERRED APHRODISIAC)

YOUR bODY: YOU de-SIDECAR

- SHAKE · SERVE UP ·

BIRTH CONTROL

BIRTH COINTREAU'L (SIDECAR)

I t's integral that people have control over their bodies, and sex is no exception. There have been many birth control methods over the years, going as far back as the seventh century BC, wherein honey, acacia leaves, and other plants containing spermicidal properties were used as contraceptives. While many of these methods have come and gone—oh, the days of using animal gut membrane as condoms!—the need for them will never disappear. Even with the continual development of diverse methods of birth control over the years, easy access to it remains a constant struggle.

To date, perhaps the most significant advancement toward gender equality came with the advent of the hormonal birth control pill in the early 1960s. The Pill was the first female-controlled contraception and was effective for not only preventing pregnancy but also for empowering as a tool of sexual liberation. This led to a radical shift in consciousness and, in many ways, a sexual revolution. Still, access to the Pill was scarce, and in the early days it was only legally available to (majority white) married women with written permission from their husbands. As birth control has become more widely available and destigmatized, the number of unintended pregnancies has massively reduced, as have abortion procedures.

Besides reducing pregnancy, birth control is the best way to prevent the spread of sexually transmitted diseases between partners—the condom being the most effective one. So, let's get this straight: With birth control you can have sex for pleasure, fewer STDs hanging out in your crotch, and more control over your own reproductive system and future?! In-condom-ceivable!

Drink this cocktail and wet your whistle by yourself, with another person, or with several. They say alcohol is a social lubricant, after all. . . .

SUSAN SONTAG

SU-SAZERAC SONTAG (SAZERAC)

Be serious, be passionate, wake up.   —Susan Sontag

Susan Sontag was an American academic, activist, and author, with a Renaissance approach to her work and life. A brilliant scholar, she graduated from the University of Chicago at eighteen and then pursued graduate work at Harvard University and St. Anne's College at Oxford. She published her first novel, *The Benefactor*, in 1963, but it was her 1964 essay "Notes on 'Camp'" that earned her literary notoriety. In it, she addressed ideas about what kind of art could be considered culturally significant and elevated pop culture while doing so. She went on to write more than a dozen books, including the National Book Award–winning *In America*. Her artistic reach also stretched to the stage and the film worlds.

Sontag was one of the most influential critics in twentieth-century thought and helped illuminate the spaces where art, history, memory, sex, and politics intersect. She often revisited the conceptual groundings of photography, exploring the various ways we experience the world around us. Her insightful essay collection *On Photography* was remarkable for its insight into the visual overload of the digital age, more than four decades ago. Susan Sontag left behind an impressive body of work that solidified her as one of the most prominent American critics of all time. Talk about a hard Sazer-act to follow!

Picture this: you mix up the perfect Sazerac after carefully examining how each of the components exists in space and how they are perceived when their paths intersect; you take a photograph of it because it looks so damn sexy; you taste it and observe how your senses perceive the cocktail differently; you try not to be absinthe-minded; you down the drink; you reminisce on the experience of it alongside its photograph; you get drunk and Sazer-act a fool.

MULLED

INCITE!r
WOMEN OF COLOR AGAINST VIOLENCE

IN A SAUCEPAN

Served in mugs
Serves 4-6

* 1 gallon jug fresh apple cider
* baking spices to taste: cloves, star anise, nutmeg
* 4 cinnamon sticks

Simmer for 20 minutes...

* 1½ oz brandy
* ½ oz Root Liqueur (optional)
* top with cider

garnish with 1 cinnamon stick

we're grass-rooting for you!

INCITE!

MULLED INCITE!'R (BRANDY MULLED CIDER)

W hat began as a small conference in 2000 ("The Color of Violence: Violence Against Women of Color," at the University
of California, Santa Cruz) has grown into an extensive and
inclusive movement to end violence against women of color using the
tools of critical dialogue, grassroots organization, and direct action.

At the 2000 conference, speaker Angela Davis asked, "How do we
develop analyses and organizing strategies against violence against
women that acknowledge the race of gender and the gender of race?"
INCITE! answered by tackling the thorny and politically uncomfort-
able issues that more mainstream, corporatized organizations could
not or would not address vigorously enough to protect women of
color.

INCITE! takes a broad-based stand by addressing the violence that
permeates communities of color from the outside, such as attacks on
immigrant rights, police brutality, and for-profit prisons, as well as
from within communities of color, in the form of hate crimes against
queer women of color, rape, and domestic violence. The group's efforts
work outside of the typical nonprofit funding system by refusing government grants. But that hasn't stopped grassroots organization that
has seen chapters across the country take direct action for the empowerment and in the defense of women of color.

*INCITE! is what unstoppable grassroots organizing is, to a tea! Or to a cider.
It's time to organize and get ex-cidered about creating dialogue, organizing
with direct action, and imagining a future devoid of hate crimes and violence
against women, people of color, and the queer communities. Do you really
need to mull this over?*

WINE, BEER & CIDER

Rosé the Riveter

in a wineglass with ice

- 4 oz AMERICAN ROSÉ*
- ½ oz APEROL
- top with club soda

GARNISH with the most CORN-SYRUP-brined, bright Red AMERICAN MARASCHINO CHERRY YOU CAN find

* the quality of American wine has vastly improved in recent years, and with more producers employing sustainable methods & practices, it's easy to find an affordable option (try a grenache blend from California's Central Valley or a Pinot Noir from the Finger Lakes of New York).

ROSIE THE RIVETER

ROSÉ THE RIVETER (ROSÉ SPRITZER)

This babe is one of the most recognizable and significant symbolic female icons in American history. When the United States entered World War II in 1941, millions of men enlisted as soldiers, leaving a substantial gap in the workforce. Using glamorized propaganda, government and industrial leaders called on American women to fulfill their "civic duty" to join the workforce and take jobs in factories—including the production of munitions and war supplies. Although Rosie's image was created as propaganda, the mere suggestion of a strong woman icon redefined what, up to that point, had been a single conventional role. At the time, this was a huge step in challenging the traditional roles of women, as well as shifting women's perceptions of themselves. In the 1970s, the image of Rosie the Riveter was adopted and reclaimed by feminist movements, and she continues to be used as a modern symbol of female empowerment. This most iconic portrait of Rosie is still celebrated and frequently imitated in pop culture. From celebrities like Beyoncé using the pose to political artists drawing it with the likeness of the *Star Wars* heroine Princess Leia, leader of the resistance, the World War II Rosie the Riveter icon has evolved into a symbol of a strong, independent heroine and one who is ready to kick some ass.

Make this drink at home. Or at work. Or anywhere you feel like. You can do it! Go on, flex your muscles, lift your glass—that's the Spritz!

eLLA
BA-KIR ROYALE

IN A FLUTE

½ oz Crème de Cassis

top with
4-5 oz CHAMPAGNE (OR ANY DRY SPARKLING WINE)

GARNISH WITH
A SLICE OF
N·A·A·C·Peach
&
A FRESH BERRY

N·A·A·C·P

FR3EDM

ELLA BAKER

ELLA BA-KIR ROYALE (KIR ROYALE)

Until the killing of black men, black mothers' sons, becomes as important to the rest of the country as the killing of a white mother's son, we who believe in freedom cannot rest.

—Ella Baker

Ella Baker was a lifelong fighter for civil rights and the greater representation of women in social movements. Her advocacy work was seen by many as the backbone of the Civil Rights Movement and earned her the nickname "Fundi," a Swahili word that denotes someone who passes knowledge from generation to generation.

In 1943, Baker was named the director of branches for the NAACP, making her the highest-ranking woman at that time. She joined the Southern Christian Leadership Conference (SCLC) in 1957 and helped guide the Student Nonviolent Coordinating Committee (SNCC). In 1962, she joined the Southern Conference Educational Fund (SCEF) to work across racial lines for social justice and to educate southern whites about the effects of racism. Baker also led some of the first civil rights boycotts of segregated public buses and helped found and organize the Freedom Rides. These actions eventually forced the Interstate Commerce Commission to implement desegregation on their buses. Baker's leadership encouraged subsequent advocacy campaigns during the civil rights era and beyond, inspiring courageous freedom fighters everywhere.

This is an Ella'f a cocktail. The backbone of this cocktail is the crème de cassis, which adds complexity without entirely stealing the show. Now crème'mber, stay currant, stay informed, and always stay tipsy!

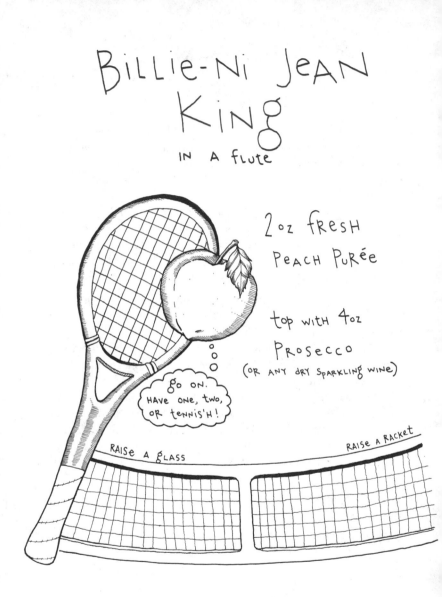

BILLIE JEAN KING

BILLIE-NI JEAN KING (BELLINI)

Ever since that day when I was eleven years old and I wasn't allowed in a photo because I wasn't wearing a tennis skirt, I knew that I wanted to change the sport.

—Billie Jean King

For the better part of a decade (between 1966 and 1975), Billie Jean King was the best women's tennis player in the world. And she was definitely not afraid to make a racket. In a time of sweeping societal change, she became a champion on and off the court by taking on equal rights and equal pay for women.

In 1973, Bobby Riggs, a former tennis champion, challenged King to a "Battle of the Sexes." Riggs claimed the women's game was so inferior that even a fifty-five-year-old guy like him could beat their best. King set him straight, 6–4, 6–3, 6–3, in front of a television audience of ninety million worldwide. (And she took home a hundred thousand dollars to boot!)

In 1981, King was outed as a lesbian in a palimony suit, marking her as one of the first openly gay professional athletes. Forced out of the closet, King refused to be victimized and instead decided to fight the public defamation against her. She used the opportunity to openly advocate for the rights of the lesbian, gay, bisexual, and transgender community and would continue that work for decades to come. As a token of appreciation and acknowledgment, she was awarded the Presidential Medal of Freedom in 2009.

Billie've in the impossible: the game may be (Bobby) Rigged, but if you work at it, you can outsmart it and win. The ball's in your court.

Margaret Sanger-ia

IN A PITCHER
(Serves 2-4)

- 1 bottle dry Red wine (750 ML)
- ½ cup brandy
- ¼ cup gin
- ¼ cup Cointreau
- ½ cup orange juice
- 2 tbsp sugar
- 2 cups assorted fruit, sliced & chopped (oranges, grapes, plums, pineapple & apples all work... to your health!

° Stir ° Serve Over Ice °

MARGARET SANGER

MARGARET SANGER-IA (SANGRIA)

*Against the State, against the Church, against the silence of
the medical profession, against the whole machinery of dead
institutions of the past, the woman of today arises.*

—Margaret Sanger

At the forefront of the crusade for accessible birth control was Margaret Sanger. This fiercely independent obstetrics nurse from Brooklyn, New York, believed that contraceptives weren't just a practical necessity but a human right. For years, she witnessed the suffering of women who had to endure unwanted pregnancies or dangerous, botched self-inflicted abortions. In 1916, she illegally opened the first birth control clinic in the United States, where she distributed diaphragms and informational pamphlets (*What Every Girl Should Know*). Despite being imprisoned and criticized for encouraging lewd behavior, Sanger dedicated herself to this cause and helped found the American Birth Control League, which was the precursor to Planned Parenthood. She also sought out researchers to establish the earliest available oral contraceptive, which completely changed the conversation around a woman's sexuality and control over her own body. Even though the Pill was originally only prescribed to married women, it eventually became more widely available due in no small part to Sanger's work. Still, we're a long way from seeing her work fully carried out, with access to birth control and funding for clinics being cut all the time due to efforts that suppress a woman's right to have control over her own body. Don't despair—let us instead Sang'er praises and continue her fight!

Margaret a load of this: this cocktail verges on being healthy, since it's loaded with fresh fruit. And since wine is made from grapes, you're basically just having a fruit salad. Do it for your body—you'll feel Sangereat!

Women in the Mili-Sherry Cobbler

in a Highball (or Canteen)

4 oz Sherry (Amontillado is best)

2 tbsp Sugar

¼ oz Lemon Juice

2 Orange Slices

- Hard Shake to bruise the oranges.
- Strain. Serve over crushed (or boot-stomped) Ice
- Garnish with fresh berries & orange slice

⚓ Optional Navy-Strength Rum Float on top

... but save a few Rounds for Later

WOMEN IN THE MILITARY

WOMEN IN THE MILI-SHERRY COBBLER (SHERRY COBBLER)

*If members of our military can meet the qualifications for a job,
then they should have the right to serve, regardless of creed,
color, gender or sexual orientation.*
       —Leon E. Panetta, former U.S. secretary of defense

Women have served in the military for as long as there have been wars to be fought. In America, Deborah Sampson famously disguised herself as a man while serving seventeen months of combat duty in the Colonial Army. During the Civil War, four hundred women took up arms. In World War I, more than twenty-five thousand served as nurses or support staff. World War II saw that number quintuple. However, it wasn't until 1948 that women could receive veterans' benefits, and it took until 1976 for women to be allowed entry into the military academies where the top brass are made. And, while women were officially held out of combat duty by the Ground Combat Exclusion Policy (GCEP), the fuzzy lines between combat and noncombat roles in modern warfare have seen a generation of women risk life and limb in service without credit. In January 2016, however, the GCEP was lifted, in part because of a lawsuit brought by Mary Jennings Hegar and the ACLU, which called the exclusion of women from combat unconstitutional. Despite your stance on war, we salute the women warriors who have been on the front lines of this gradual change to help arm future soldiers with more opportunities and greater respect. It was definitely time for change—those old laws were totally out of WAC.

Pass your canteen (filled with this drink, obviously) to your mate and remind them you're in this together—you know what they say: a problem sherry'd is a problem halved. Be their soldier to cry on. And, yes, if everyone wants to put down their weapons—man and woman alike—that's cool, too.

SOJU-OURNER TRUTH

TRUTH BOMB!

IN A PINT GLASS & SHOT GLASS

- 3/4 - FULL PINT GLASS OF LAGER
- 1 1/4 OZ KOREAN SOJU
  IN A SHOT GLASS

DROP SOJU IN
&
CHUG IT ALL DOWN

SOJOURNER TRUTH

SOJU-OURNER TRUTH BOMB (SOJU BOMB)

I have plowed and planted and gathered into barns, and no man could head me. And aren't I a woman?

—Sojourner Truth

Sojourner Truth was one of America's most prominent abolitionists and advocates for women's rights. In 1826, she escaped slavery with her infant daughter by accepting shelter in New Paltz, New York, but was forced to leave behind three of her children. When she learned that her son had been sold to a slave owner in Alabama, she took the case to court and won his freedom. That victory marked one of the first times in a U.S. court that a black woman prevailed over a white man.

Truth spoke at the first National Woman's Rights Convention in 1850, which led to regular speaking engagements where she discussed human rights and slavery. In 1851, she gave her best-known speech, the extemporaneous "Ain't I a Woman" talk, at the Ohio Women's Rights Convention. One of her greatest weapons against the injustice of the institution of slavery was her ability to unite people through songs and hymns with messages of shared struggle.

During the Civil War, Truth actively recruited black troops for the Union and contributed to the National Freedman's Relief Association. Truth continued the fight for the rights of freedmen and -women well after the war, pushing for prison reform, property rights, and universal suffrage until her death in 1883.

Soju, the Korean clear distilled liquor that, at first glance, seems like a docile, even harmlessly sippable spirit, will knock you on your ass. Drop a shot directly into a frosty pint, and you'll be dropping truth bombs that are so electrifying, everyone around you will be rallying behind your cause.

MICHELLE-ADA OBAMA

IN A HIGHBALL

feel free to swap out for a pint glass & add more beer

- 3-4 oz tomato or vegetable juice
  (extra credit if you blend or juice your own fresh veggies)
- 2+ dashes Hot Sauce to taste
- 2 dashes Worcestershire Sauce
- 2 dashes Maggi seasoning or Soy Sauce
- Top with Light beer (Presidente, perhaps?)
- * Lime wedge & a spicy pepper

When they go low, we go highball

A few ice cubes o Chili Salt Rim

MICHELLE OBAMA

MICHELLE-ADA OBAMA (MICHELADA)

Besides her being the United States's forty-fourth First Lady, and the first black woman to hold that position, Michelle Obama's advocacy work—on a local, national, and international level—has been thoroughly impressive. Raised in Chicago's South Side, Obama began building herself as an activist at an early age. During her Princeton days, she participated in local demonstrations, grassroots organizing, and public affairs. She met her future husband, Barack, while mentoring him at a law firm in Chicago. As a team, they would go on to campaign and fund-raise as he built his career in politics.

After having their two daughters, Malia and Sasha, Obama made her family her top priority. As First Lady, her previous activism efforts helped shape her focus on public advocacy concerning nutrition, education, race, and equal opportunity, culminating most famously with her Let's Move! campaign, which worked to bring awareness to the dangers of childhood obesity and malnutrition. Perhaps the most unique and lasting aspect of her legacy is that she used her platform to encourage and inspire children, with a particular focus on empowering young girls. In her final days in the White House, Obama urged Americans to stay tough and fearless, and to "be focused. Be determined. Be hopeful. . . . Lead by example." I elect to drink to that!

Check out what delicious veggies are in season from your local farmers' market or grocery store, blend or juice them up with some spicy fixin's, add some beer (naturally), and make Obama Mama proud!

If you want to really pump up this drink with nutrients, throw in a shot of wheatgrass—it puts the "grass" in "grassroots"! Okay, there's a good chance that won't taste very good, so parsley is a fine alternative. It puts the "par" in "achieving bipartisanship through determination and understanding."

SUSAN B. ANTHONY

SAISON BEER ANTHONY (SHANDY)

It was we, the people; not we, the white male citizens; nor yet we, the male citizens; but we, the whole people, who formed the Union.

—Susan B. Anthony

Susan B. Anthony was one of the great crusaders of the early women's suffrage movement in the United States. Born in Massachusetts in 1820 to an activist Quaker family, she was raised to be acutely aware of the injustices of slavery and became an ardent abolitionist. A passionate and skilled orator, Anthony knew how to appeal to people's common sense and compassion. In one of her first public attempts to point out hypocrisy within government, Anthony and fifteen other women were arrested for voting illegally in an election in 1872, arguing that it was their right under the Fourteenth Amendment. Together with Elizabeth Cady Stanton, another prominent crusader, Anthony pushed for additional rights, advocating for laws that would provide women with greater economic independence, increased property privileges, and control of their own earnings.

After the Civil War ended, Anthony continued to fight for the right to vote, urging fellow abolitionists to join her in trying to amend the law to include women in addition to black men. Anthony wouldn't live to see women achieve suffrage, unfortunately, but no doubt she helped set it into motion.

Pubs are public houses, and public houses are community centers. It's only natural that Anthony's drink should be a sessionable beer: the official drink of a pub, since she really knew how to bring people together and rally behind a cause. Okay, she didn't drink and was even part of the Temperance Movement, but that shouldn't leave a sour taste in your mouth!

BURN YOUR BRA'SS MONKEY

IN A PINT GLASS
(OR TWO JUGS)

- POUR 1/4 GLASS FULL OF ORANGE JUICE

- FILL REMAINDER OF GLASS WITH A LIGHT BEER OR MALT LIQUOR

- ORANGE SLICE SOAKED IN 151-PROOF RUM PLACE ON RIM OF THE GLASS & LIGHT ON FIRE (OR DON'T)

FREEDOM TRASH CAN

QUICKLY EXTINGUISH & WAIT FOR PEOPLE TO START TALKING

BURNING BRAS

BURN YOUR BRA'SS MONKEY (BRASS MONKEY)

In the late 1960s and early 1970s, it is said that some women publicly burned their bras to send a message to the world about the way women's bodies were treated as sexual objects. It was a theatrical protest tactic, a performance that used an element of the spectacular and the provocative to convey a political message. Bra burning was a symbolic rejection of what many women believed was a patriarchal imprisonment of their own bodies and femininity.

The first known bra burning was in 1968, when activists, students, and individuals from women's liberation groups rallied at the Miss America pageant in Atlantic City. This was the most famous mention of a bra burning; however, it was said to have been fabricated for newspaper headlines, and no bras were actually burned that day. The protesters instead threw bras, girdles, lipstick, sanitary napkins, high heels, and other items of female oppression into a symbolic "freedom trash can." Whether or not anyone's over-the-shoulder-boulder-holder was set on fire that day or at other demonstrations to follow, the important thing to take away is that women were challenging and rejecting sexist beauty ideals and social expectations. The media galvanized (you could even say "ignited") the conversation among everyday Americans, but in the process, it also trivialized the true significance of the message. Regardless of the joking tone taken by the media, the coverage helped bring attention to many women's dissatisfaction with archaic beauty standards and catalyzed a bigger conversation. You know what they say: there's no smoke without fire—and there's nothing like a flammable polyester bra, doused in symbolic femininity, to really heat things up.

Now don't you have a burning desire to try this drink? Admit it, you love cheap beer. Doesn't it feel good to get that off your chest? We're here to lift one another up for support, after all!

the ORIGINALLY Sinful Snakebite

IN A PINT GLASS

FILL HALFWAY WITH LAGER &
HALFWAY WITH HARD APPLE CIDER

FLOAT ~1 OZ CRÈME de CASSIS
(BLACK CURRANT LIQUEUR —
OR ANY FORBIDDEN
FRUIT CORDIAL OR LIQUEUR)

A'DAM
fine DRINK

EVE - RYONE
AGREES

EVE

THE ORIGINALLY SINFUL SNAKEBITE (SNAKEBITE)

This snake bites back! —Eve, probably

Eve, in biblical folklore, was the first woman, created from Adam's rib by God. Religious scholars argue over the relevance of this act. Was Eve conjured from the rib as a protected subordinate or from his side as an equal? Perhaps she is instead the perfected half of the pair? After all, if God distilled Adam from the earth, does this not make Eve twice distilled, therefore purer in essence and form?

To complicate things even more, God named Eve Adam's "helper," and again scholars find debate in the language. Where does this place Eve's station relative to Adam? Does "helper" mean a leading guide or a mere assistant? The patriarchy has its ideas, feminists their own.

Then there's the Fall of Man, spearheaded by Eve's temptation by the serpent, Satan in disguise. Deceived into tasting fruit (an apple, to be exact) from the Tree of Knowledge, Adam blames Eve, and both are expelled from Eden and doomed to mortality. Still, Eve takes the worst of it, sentenced to pain in childbirth and subservience to Adam.

Whatever the version, Eve's (or "Man's") notorious creation story is the most significant on gender in the long, complex narrative of Western history. And one that has informed virtually every patriarchal-prescribed notion of woman and morality.

Or maybe the Gnostics have it right and Eve is the incarnation of the feminine principle. Who knows? I guess it will always remain a mystery-Eve.

Try to find a nice garden to enjoy this refreshing drink, but be wary of snakes in the grass who want to steal a taste. No matter how apple-ing his argument, don't Eden think about sharing—better yet, chug the whole drink and then ask him, "How do you like them apples?"

OTHER SPIRITS

FR'ANGELA DAVIS

IN A MUG

- 1 oz Irish whiskey
- 1 oz Frangelico
- ½ oz Irish Cream Liqueur
- 1 cup strong black coffee

• Stir • best served Hot —
Like Right Meow!

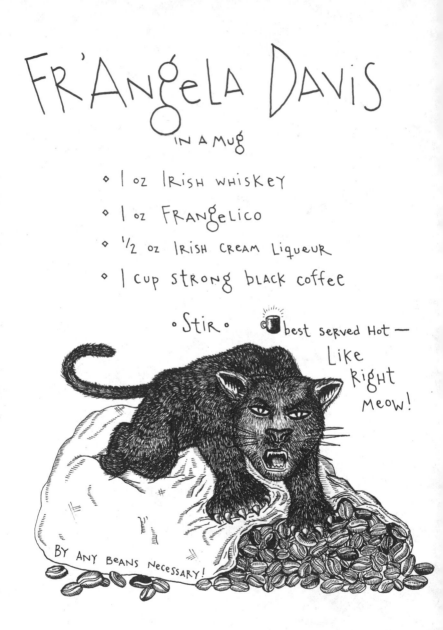

BY ANY BEANS NECESSARY!

ANGELA DAVIS

FR'ANGELA DAVIS (FRANGELICO & COFFEE)

I am no longer accepting the things I cannot change. I am changing the things I cannot accept.

—Angela Davis

Angela Davis is the quintessential activist: she has advocated for the equal rights of women, people of color, and the disenfranchised for more than fifty years. Her fearless voice has boomed since the 1960s, when the country, and much of the world, was in a state of upheaval and awakening. As a radical activist and philosopher, she has played many roles in American political culture: at one time, she was on the FBI's Ten Most Wanted Fugitives list for her affiliation with the Black Panthers (a group formed in response to centuries of violence and racism toward black men and women, and often associated with its militant approach to action); she has been a staunch advocate for the abolition of prisons; for decades, she has been one of the most well-respected university professors in the world; she's been a leader of the U.S. Communist Party, concerned with class struggle and equal rights for all; and she is a passionate poet and artist. One particularly awesome position that Davis has taken is to urge the use of "love" in bringing people together to create alternative, liberated spaces outside of the oppressive structures within class, capitalism, race, and even family. Love, compassion, and liberation? She may be onto something.

There is no better drink to cheers such an empowering woman than one that wakes you the hell up! A cup of strong black coffee—with some sugar and some booze—will remind you what the jolt is for. Be tough as nails so you can fight for the finer things: a bit of sweetness, a bit of poetry, a bit of a buzz, a bit of love. This drink is looking out for you—it's your own guardian Angela. Now pour yourself another, and seize the Davis!

MARiE CuR-ing
A HANGOVER
iN A PiNT gLASS

1 oz PeRNod AbSiNtHe

1 oz LiMe JuiCe

1 oz SiMple SyRup

4-6 oz STiLL wATeR

gARNiSH wiTH cUCuMBeR SLiceS

∘ STiR ∘ SeRve over Ice ∘

IF ALL ELSe FAiLS, dRiNK wATeR, TAKe AN ASPiRiN & eAT NACHOS

ASPiRiN
℞

MARIE CURIE

MARIE CUR-ING A HANGOVER (PUNCH)

One never notices what has been done; one can only see what remains to be done.
    —Marie Curie

Born in Poland in 1867, Marie Curie was a revered chemist and physicist whose research into radioactivity led to, among other achievements, the discovery of two elements: polonium and radium. These discoveries were crucial to the development of X-rays, specifically with regards to surgery. During World War I, Curie worked with the International Red Cross to utilize the newly formed X-ray equipment on the front lines. In addition to her advocacy, she became a crucial figure in training nurses and doctors on the new treatment techniques.

These scientific feats led to her being awarded two Nobel Prizes within her lifetime. She was the first woman to win this award and, to date, the only woman to win twice. Yet, within her career, Curie also struggled with male opposition from within her field, and she conducted her research and findings with minimal financial support, instead directing money back into scientific institutions. Her utter devotion to her studies ultimately led to her death in 1934 from leukemia, inflicted from her constant exposure to radiation—a side effect unbeknownst to the medical world at that time. Curie's legacy has helped establish her as one of the most influential scientists of all time, so let's all raise a test tube to her! Or a glass!

Is this cocktail going to cure your hangover? There's only one X-ray to find out. Make a punch bowl of this for you and your crew, and I guarantee it will save you a trip to the pharmacy. Think about it: you can't get a hangover if you never stop drinking. Chem-mystery solved!

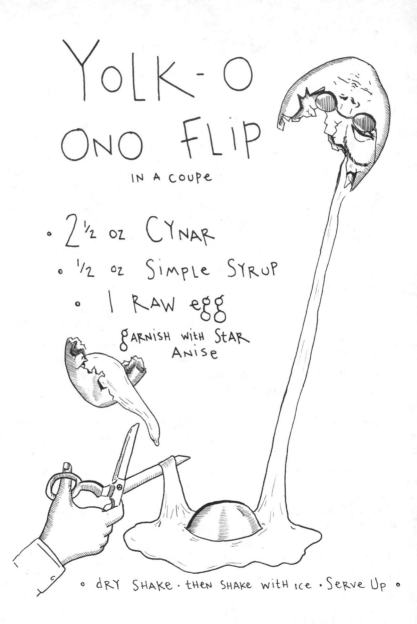

YOLK-O ONO FLIP

IN A COUPE

- 2½ oz CYNAR
- ½ oz Simple Syrup
- 1 RAW egg

GARNISH WITH STAR ANISE

○ DRY SHAKE · THEN SHAKE WITH ICE · SERVE UP ○

YOKO ONO

Art is like breathing to me. If I don't do it I start to choke.

—Yoko Ono

Born into an aristocratic Tokyo family in 1933, Yoko Ono grew up to become a controversial feminist figure. After moving to New York in the early 1960s, Ono's artistic career gained attention with her *Cut Piece* performance, wherein she invited her audience to cut off her clothes onstage. This performance was, among other things, a commentary on the role the female body has been given in art and society as a whole: something to be unveiled, objectified, and both passively and aggressively consumed.

Despite her artistic accomplishments, Ono is perhaps best known for her marriage to John Lennon of the Beatles. As a couple, they created many collaborative projects and advocated for world peace, yet the media also portrayed their marriage in a negative light, blaming her for the dissolution of the Beatles. Her continued activism and prolific artistic work in the decades since have defied that conversation and defined her contribution to the feminist cause. Through interviews, writings, and music, Yoko Ono has testified against these attacks and prejudices propagated by the media, juxtaposing her treatment with the plight of all women who face intense and unfair scrutiny. Retrospectives worldwide have helped to cement her legacy, and she continues to create, produce, and execute art that provokes the viewer.

You may be thinking, "O-no! I am not consuming a raw egg in my drink!" Sure, it may seem a bit eggs-treme, scandalous, and even dangerous, but come on, all the best art is. Let it beat. Let it beat. Just try it; Cynar you want to.

PIMM'S DIVACUP

IN A GOBLET

- 2 oz PIMM'S No. 1
- 3 oz GINGER ALE OR ANY LEMON SODA
- 1 OR 2 CUCUMBER SLICES
- ½ BLOOD ORANGE SLICE

(OPTIONAL: FOR A SLIGHTLY SWEETER, MORE COLORFUL COCKTAIL, ADD A SPLASH OF GRENADINE)

Serve over Ice

HEY, GUESS WHAT?

YOUR BODY ISN'T GROSS!

AND NEITHER IS THIS COCKTAIL

Period.

DIVACUP (MENSTRUAL CUP)

PIMM'S DIVACUP (PIMM'S CUP)

There are several brands that manufacture reusable menstrual cups, the DivaCup being one of the most well-known. It's a small rubber cup that is manually placed on the cervix and collects menstrual blood during your period. It's totally safe, easy to use, comfortable, and sanitary when properly cared for. It's also reusable and can last years, which cuts down on unnecessary waste from tampons and pads (which often contain harmful chemicals and bleach)—not to mention saves you a fortune in the long run. It may seem a little off-putting at first; to some, maybe even gross, since it totally goes against what we've always been told to believe about menstrual blood: it's disgusting, dirty, even shameful. And though this product may not be for everyone, at least it serves as a reminder that having your period is natural and healthy and beautiful. Why is it such a taboo? Talk about it; remind the girls and guys around you that it's the most natural and unifying thing we have as humans, and that's pretty fucking cool. Is it a coincidence that James Pimm, the creator of the beloved Pimm's No. 1 in the 1840s, owned several oyster bars in London? And that oysters are the best-known aphrodisiacs and the most reminiscent of the female form? Okay, yeah, it definitely is. Just remember, it's natural and nothing to be ashamed of . . . and that's a fact, not just a matter of o-Pimm-ion.

You can drink this cocktail year-round, not just at "that time of the month." Try preparing and serving it in a reusable glass rather than plastic or Styrofoam. Don't forget, the Diva's in the details.

Blue St. Ger-Moon Stockings

IN A ROCKS GLASS

- 2 oz Rye Whiskey
- 1/2 oz Amaro Montenegro
  OR A softer, less bitter Amaro
- 1/4 oz St. Germain
- 1 oz Lemon Juice
- 4 dashes Orange bitters

  freeze blueberries in ice cubes *that's AMARO!*
  Garnish with lemon twist

- SHAKE • Serve over blueberry rocks •

BLUESTOCKINGS

BLUE ST. GER-MOON STOCKINGS (AMARO SOUR)

In a woman's education little but outward accomplishment is regarded. . . . It is in the nature of mankind to hazard their peace to secure power, and they know fools make the best slaves.

—Elizabeth Montagu

In mid-eighteenth-century England, women were discouraged from pursuing formal education. It was "unbecoming" to read Greek or Latin, as needlework and knitting were considered the height of achievement. Enter the Blue Stockings Society to shake things up. Founders Elizabeth Montagu and Elizabeth Vesey formed a social club and political movement, holding meetings for women to support one another in pursuit of education, authorship, and the arts. These salons featured deep conversation among women, as well as male intellectuals who were invited to participate as equals.

The origins of the society's name are unknown, but it's speculated that it was a way of recognizing the need to promote women's education for all, regardless of class or setting. The metaphor was that black stockings were reserved for formal wear, but blue stockings could be worn whenever, wherever. Or maybe it was the intoxicating elderberry flavor that simply Blue their socks off. Discuss and get back to us.

This drink is just the right balance of subversive, fun, and challenging. Start a book club, turn your living room into an eighteenth-century-style salon, whip up a few of these cocktails, recommend a loose dress code of blue stockings, and watch the room light up. Plus, you'll be getting drunk to boot (or to sock)!

Florence Nightcap-ingale

IN A ROCKS GLASS

Stir

☆	1	oz	Cognac
☆	1	oz	Sweet Vermouth
☆	1	oz	Amaro Averna

Serve on the Rocks

Note on Nightcaps

3 of the most beloved nightcap spirits — Vermouth, Cognac & Amaro — are all, on their own, liqueurs with flavors & ingredients that are said to promote digestion, making them popular after-dinner drinks. These heavy hitters have helped shape some of the world's greatest cocktails but traditionally are often enjoyed on their own; neat or on the rocks.

VERMOUTH: An aromatized wine & an essential ingredient to cocktails. On its own, can be an elegant sipper & great nightcap.

COGNAC: A robust blend of brandies, aged & derived of grapes from a demarcated region in France.

AMARO: An Italian digestif. These are spirit-based bitters, distilled with a myriad of herbs, spices, plants & aromatics. A bittersweet end to the day.

FLORENCE NIGHTINGALE

FLORENCE NIGHTCAP-INGALE (AFTER-DINNER DRINK)

I attribute my success to this—I never gave or took any excuse.
—Florence Nightingale

F lorence Nightingale earned her legacy during the Crimean War in the 1850s. Notable for her tireless service as the "Lady with the Lamp," she led a revolution in nursing and patient care that saved countless lives. Her reform-minded actions changed the care of wounded soldiers forever.

A daughter of English privilege, Nightingale benefited from a classical education and took to philanthropic care of the poor from an early age. She rejected family and cultural expectations to marry young and instead announced her intention to become a nurse, an occupation that suffered the public perception of being made up of foul-mouthed drunks with a lax attitude toward their patients, due in large part to Sarah Gamp, the gin-swilling nurse found in Charles Dickens's *Martin Chuzzlewit*.

After the Crimean War, she used her influence to establish proper nurse training through donations gifted to the Nightingale Fund. The Nightingale Training School educated nurses in her methods and began tending to the least fortunate found in British workhouses in the 1860s.

Italian amari, which are the country's most common digestifs, translates to "bitter," but it sounds an awful lot like "amore," which means "love." Love is bittersweet, like the last drink of the night. Now take off your thinking cap, put on your nightcap, and live for today, for amaro may never come! If you happen to find yourself Cognac-ing your brains out the next morning, don't be bitter—nurse yourself back to health with a short glass: it just might cure what Nighting'ails ya.

RESOURCES

It's never too late to get involved, begin volunteering, or pick up new skills and knowledge. A movement needs people to power it, so don't feel discouraged because others have been doing it longer or have more experience being active in organizations or causes. Part of building the community and society we want to see is breaking out of our hyper-individualized mind-sets and realizing that our struggles are shared, even if they're not entirely similar. Interconnectedness, solidarity, and collective organizing can break us out of patterns of alienation and ego—which probably got us into these predicaments to begin with.

The following are a few suggestions for ways to get involved or learn more about topics discussed throughout the book, including some of the organizations that women in this book helped to herald. I've included some of my personal favorite New York City community spaces that have provided me with resources over the years (I left out the bars because, well, there are bars everywhere, and a bar can be an effective community space wherever you are in the world, if you utilize it as such), but mostly this is a broad, more general list.

I've also included a few websites that will help you locate community spaces or organizations close to you. In addition to getting involved through organizations, remember that you can use social media to circulate information, advocate for various groups, show support for causes, and tweet at or e-mail your local politicians and representatives.

This is by no means a comprehensive guide, but more of a jumping-off point. There are endless things you can do to make a change, take a stand, and support your community.

*Referenced specifically in this book

Women's Health and Reproductive Rights
- Planned Parenthood,* www.plannedparenthood.org
- Center for Reproductive Rights, www.reproductiverights.org
- *Hot Pantz*: DIY gynecology zine

- Let's Move!,* letsmove.obamawhitehouse.archives.gov
- National Association for the Repeal of Abortion Laws (NARAL) Pro-Choice America,* www.prochoiceamerica.org
- Our Bodies Ourselves (OBOS),* www.ourbodiesourselves.org
- Reproductive Health Access Project, www.reproductiveaccess.org
- Sex Workers Outreach Project (SWOP), www.new.swopusa.org

Protecting Civil Liberties and the Rights of Women
- American Association of People with Disabilities (AAPD), www.aapd.com
- American Civil Liberties Union (ACLU),* www.aclu.org
- Communities United for Police Reform, www.changethenypd.org
- Council on American-Islamic Relations (CAIR), www.cair.com
- Critical Resistance, www.criticalresistance.org
- Democracy at Work, www.democracyatwork.info
- Global Fund for Women, www.globalfundforwomen.org
- Human Rights Watch, www.hrw.org
- Let Girls Learn, www.letgirlslearn.gov
- Malala Fund,* www.malala.org
- MoveOn.org, www.moveon.org
- National Organization for Women (NOW),* www.now.org
- National Women's Law Center, www.nwlc.org
- Rainbow PUSH Coalition (RPC), www.rainbowpush.org
- Service Women's Action Network (SWAN), www.servicewomen.org
- Women's March,* www.womensmarch.com
- Women's Sports Foundation, www.womenssportsfoundation.org

Support for Victims of Sexual Assault and Violence
- Amber Rose SlutWalk,* www.amberroseslutwalk.com
- INCITE! Women, Gender Non-Conforming, and Trans People of Color Against Violence,* www.incite-national.org
- National Coalition Against Domestic Violence (NCADV), www.ncadv.org
- New York City Alliance Against Sexual Assault, www.svfreenyc.org
- Rape, Abuse & Incest National Network (RAINN), www.rainn.org; crisis hotline: 800-656-4673
- SafeHorizon, www.safehorizon.org
- Take Back the Night (TBTN),* www.takebackthenight.org
- UltraViolet, www.weareultraviolet.org

Rights of Workers, Immigrants, and Indigenous Communities
- Chiapas Support Committee,* www.chiapas-support.org
- Sparrow Charitable Fund (Hooligan Sparrow),* www.hooliganspar row.com/sparrow-charitable-fund
- Industrial Workers of the World (IWW), www.iww.org
- Native American Rights Fund, www.narf.org
- National Immigration Law Center, www.nilc.org
- United Farm Workers (formerly National Farm Workers Association),* www.ufw.org

Protecting and Supporting People of Color
- Black Lives Matter, www.blacklivesmatter.com
- Campaign Zero, www.joincampaignzero.org
- Color of Change, www.colorofchange.org
- ColorComm (Women of Color in Communications), www.colorcomm network.com
- The Empowerment Program, www.empowermentprogram.org
- National Association for the Advancement of Colored People (NAACP),* www.naacp.org

Education, Libraries, and Archive Centers
- American Alliance of Museums, aam-us.org
- American Association of University Women (AAUW), www.aauw.org
- Amy Poehler's Smart Girls, www.amysmartgirls.com
- Institute of Museum and Library Services, www.imls.gov
- National Public Radio (NPR), www.npr.org
- PEN America, www.pen.org
- Public Art Archive, www.publicartarchive.org

Protecting LGBTQ Rights
- Gay & Lesbian Alliance Against Defamation (GLAAD), www.glaad.org
- Human Rights Campaign, www.hrc.org
- Lambda Legal, www.lambdalegal.org
- Mazzoni Center, www.mazzonicenter.org
- National LGBTQ Task Force, www.thetaskforce.org
- Sylvia Rivera Law Project,* www.srlp.org

Environmental Protection
- Conservation International, www.conservation.org
- The Dian Fossey Gorilla Fund International,* www.gorillafund.org

- Environmental Defense Fund, www.edf.org
- The Green Belt Movement,* www.greenbeltmovement.org
- NextGen America, www.nextgenclimate.org
- Sierra Club, www.sierraclub.org

Additional Resources & Publications
- Bitch Media, www.bitchmedia.org
- *BUST*, www.bust.com
- Jezebel, www.jezebel.com
- *Ms.*,* www.msmagazine.com
- "Riot Grrrl Manifesto,"* www.onewarart.org/riot_grrrl_manifesto.htm

How to Find Your Local . . . (Some Useful Lists)
- Common Cause (local elected official: how to contact, information on bills, associated committees, political affiliations), www.common cause.org
- Corporation for National & Community Service, www.nationalser vice.gov
- The Leap (list of resources on how to get involved organizing around social justice issues and climate change), www.theleap.org
- Radical Reference (radical bookstore and library), www.radicalref erence.info
- VolunteerMatch, www.voluntcermatch.org

NYC Personal Favorites
- ABC No Rio (community space, venue, DIY art and activist center), www.abcnorio.org
- Babeland (sex-positive women and queer-friendly sex-toy shop), www .babeland.com
- The Base (community space and leftist activist center), thebasebk.org
- Bluestockings (bookstore, feminist activist center, and fair trade café),* www.bluestockings.com
- Interference Archive (public political art archives and community space), www.interferencearchive.org
- JustFood (food justice organization), www.justfood.org
- Mayday Community Space (venue, activist center), www.mayday space.org
- New York Cares (volunteer database), www.newyorkcares.org
- Women's Health Free Clinic (WHFC), www.nycfreeclinic.med.nyu.edu /womens-health-free-clinic

ACKNOWLEDGMENTS

This book would not exist without the support of so many invaluable people in my life. Thank you to Kate Napolitano, my brilliant and badass editor, who guided this book from its histrionic infancy to a beautiful final form. My agent, Janis Donnaud. Our meeting was pure kismet! My respect and gratitude for you is immeasurable. Thank you to Rebecca Strobel, Jason Booher, Kayleigh George, and the dream team at Plume and Penguin Random House.

To Mom, Dad, Amia, Palguna, and my Berkeley hippie family. You taught me what unconditional love is and made me think I'm really funny. My sister, Amia Grashin. You're my best friend and most honest critic.

To Stephanie Danler, for your insight, inspiration, and sunshine cave with walls made of poetry. Jane-Claire Quigley, whose bar tab for Rosé the Riveters will remain open for gifting me this spark. To Cara Nicoletti. My guiding light and my sausage queen. To my QC tester, Brett Helms. I trust you with my life and, amazingly, with my book. Joan Cone and Penny Vlagopolous, two teachers who have taught me what it is to be a radical woman. To Hewah Bahrami and Sarah Evans. My backbone, heart, and liver—my most ruthless drinking companions. I'm deeply touched by your boundless confidence in me.

For contributing edits, recipes, industry expertise, witchcraft: Jackie Little, Bonnie Pipkin, Jim Hill, Benjamin Harrison, Bryan Cerenzio, Drea Bega, Steven Ditchkus, Gavin Morse, Gregor Goldman, Austin Hartman, Andrea Savlov, BAM, '90s x, and my enormous extended bar family who have nurtured me with love, laughter, and libations.

Cheers to the women who fill these pages and who helped me sustain a thirst for learning, questioning, putting pun to paper, and, of course, drinking.

And to Valerie. Best listener, number one cuddler, cutest paws, worst breath. A real wiener in my book.